LUCKY MAN

Lucky Man

The Autobiography

Greg Lake

Constable • London

CONSTABLE

First published in Great Britain in 2017 by Constable

1 3 5 7 9 10 8 6 4 2

Copyright © Creative Musical Arts Ltd, 2017

The moral right of the author has been asserted.

A CIP catalogue record for this book
is available from the British Library.

ISBN: 978-1-47212-648-1 (hardback)
ISBN: 978-1-47212-649-8 (trade paperback)

Typeset in Bembo by SX Composing DTP, Rayleigh, Essex
Printed and bound in Great Britain by Clays Ltd, St Ives plc

Papers used by Constable are from well-managed forests
and other responsible sources.

Constable
An imprint of
Little, Brown Book Group
Carmelite House
50 Victoria Embankment
London EC4Y 0DZ

An Hachette UK Company
www.hachette.co.uk

www.littlebrown.co.uk

DEDICATION

During my lifetime I seem to have been blessed in so many different ways, but without doubt the greatest of all of these was the good fortune to have met and eventually married the love of my life, Regina, who for over forty years has stood by my side through good times and bad.

The music business is a notoriously difficult place for any marriage to survive, and it is through her good grace and strength of character that we have been able to endure and it is to her that I dedicate this book.

GREG LAKE

CONTENTS

Part Three

Madison Square Garden, 17 December 1973

This was the night that every musician in the world dreams about. Here we were, Emerson, Lake & Palmer, the three of us standing together at the bottom of the stairs to the stage, waiting for the house lights to go down and for the show to begin. The air was charged with electricity: the audience was expecting to see the greatest show of their lives.

All of a sudden, with his hands firmly gripping his headset, the stage manager turned towards us and asked if we were ready to go. We looked at each other momentarily, then gave the thumbs up. Almost immediately the house lights went down as the entire audience began to scream. Then, echoing all around the arena, came the legendary voice of the late and great Scott Muni. 'Ladies and gentlemen, now get ready!

All the way from London, England, to perform for you tonight, here they are! The fantastic, Emerson, Lake & Palmer!'

As we walked out on to the stage, the screaming turned into a thunderous avalanche that caused the 22,000-seat arena to shake to its foundations. Nothing can quite prepare you for this feeling. *This* is Madison Square Garden, New York.

We have all heard the line about New York: *If you can make it there you can make it anywhere.* When you stand on the stage at Madison Square Garden, it's like staring out at a gladiatorial arena. It's an awesome and imposing spectacle – and the New York audience is ferocious. They have seen it all, so to break through there you've got to be a little special. If they love you, they *love* you. If they don't, it's not so good! But when we played there on 17 December 1973, they loved us.

The *Brain Salad Surgery* album had been released a month earlier and to celebrate the event we had embarked upon our fifth North American tour. By now the show had evolved into a huge production. The question most bands – most great bands – ask is: how can we be better? Better songs, better sound, better visuals, better anything and everything. When you play shows in different venues every night, it all changes: the acoustics, the distance you are from each other, the lighting, everything. I thought one thing we could do was to design our own self-contained stage, with built-in monitoring, so that the sound every night would be the same – because, if the sound isn't in order, the playing never will be. Ringo Starr told me that one of the reasons the Beatles retired from live performance was because they couldn't hear what they were doing, which became too frustrating. Hearing your fellow musicians is pretty much everything when you are performing live.

That was the primary reason why we toured with our own stage set. And along with the sound, we gave a lot of thought to the visual elements that would underpin and empower the music, such as the lighting and the stunts, including Keith riding the organ, stabbing the keys and throwing daggers.

The set included an enormous circular projection screen, 156 feet in diameter. During the show, it would display eerie skull imagery from H. R. Giger, who had designed the *Brain Salad Surgery* album cover. There were two sixty-foot proscenium arches, framing the stage and holding 100 spotlights, which were assembled by our crew as part of a load-in that took five hours. Carl Palmer had developed a new hand-engraved, revolving, stainless-steel drum kit weighing in at a remarkable four tons, which by itself took a crew of six roadies over two hours to erect every night. The kit was set up within a frame styled like a Japanese pagoda and complete with thirty-eight-inch Paiste gongs and a custom-made cast-bronze church bell. With the help of our friend David Hardstone and his cutting-edge sound company, IES, we had also developed a brand new thirty-channel quadrophonic PA system with thirty-two speaker stacks weighing thirty-six tons. I had my multi-guitar rack and, of course, my $6,000 spotlit Persian rug. And Keith had a full-size Steinway grand piano, which would float up into the air before spinning around in circles, with Keith still playing it, and then disappearing into a massive cloud of smoke and flame.

That night at Madison Square Garden was one of the shows that people still come up to talk to me about to this very day. We were just entering the period that many people think of as ELP's golden era. The band was right on top of its game from a musical standpoint and at the very cutting edge of technology as well. It was also a time when the band still felt like a brotherhood – the spirit was all for one and one for all before individual egos and self-indulgence from all of us began to erode the power of the bond.

We were entertainers. Every night, we would give everything in order to entertain as much as possible, and when we came off the stage we would be so tired that we would be shaking and trembling.

As we came towards the end of the show, we performed 'Pictures at an Exhibition' and during the tubular bells section, right before the huge climax of 'The Great Gates of Kiev', we diverted away and I sang the Christmas carol 'Silent Night'. As I began to sing, the entire stage fell into darkness and, rising up from what seemed like nowhere, the Harlem Gospel Choir appeared, dressed in their maroon and white robes and joining in with their massed voices. I can still remember the hair standing up on the back of my neck. Just to add to the emotion, snow started to fall *inside* the whole of Madison Square Garden just as the last verse began.

PROLOGUE

It was probably the most spectacular single stage production I have ever been involved in. The audience went crazy and we then went on to finish the climax of 'Pictures of an Exhibition' with Keith and the grand piano spinning around in the air before disappearing in a cloud of smoke.

When the show came to an end, both the band and the audience were completely demolished. It was a magical, once-in-a-lifetime performance. I will never forget the incredible reception we received. It confirmed that New York had taken the band to its heart. Afterwards we mainly felt relief.

Aaahh. At least I don't have to go through that again.

Part One

CHAPTER 1

Opening Notes

I have always seen music as something magical. As a young boy of five or six years old, I heard the medieval tune of 'Greensleeves' playing on the radio, and I was emotionally touched by its magical power. I had heard lots of music before, of course – Vera Lynne and all that sort of stuff, which was popular at the time – but that piece taught me that music could really mean something, and that it could touch people personally. I still feel like that when I listen to similar pieces of music to this day – I think it is to do with the way they are structured: there is a feeling of suspension and then relief, which draws you in and makes you react emotionally.

Looking back, I am quite sure this is what first ignited my interest in playing the guitar. Of course, back then there was no way I could have possibly imagined the incredible journey that I was about to embark upon, or how this shapely little piece of painted wood with its six wire strings would ultimately control the destiny of my entire life.

I was born shortly after the end of the Second World War on 10 November 1947 and grew up in the small harbour town of Poole in Dorset on the south coast of England. Poole today is a modern, thriving and increasingly wealthy little harbour town with swishy yacht clubs and numerous golf courses. It's just a little way down the road from Sandbanks, known for its extraordinarily expensive houses, but once just a sleepy little retirement backwater until one fine day when a young lad called John Lennon bought his Aunt Mimi a house there. When I was a young boy growing up, Poole was nothing more than a dirty, rundown Victorian slum whose main claim to fame was its coal-fired gasworks, which nightfall somehow transformed into an eerie *Quartermass* landscape.

My grandparents lived adjacent to the gasworks in a Victorian terraced house for most of their adult lives, and my grandfather worked there until he was forced to retire with lung cancer at the age of fifty-five. The cancer was almost certainly caused by the smoke and coal dust that he was breathing in every day.

When I was seven or eight years old, I stood with my father at the main entrance to the gasworks, no doubt waiting for my grandfather to leave work. I was horrified by the overwhelming stench of gas that hung in the air and by the huge mountains of coal that glittered in the orange flames that burned continually day and night. I thought that if there was a place called hell, then this was probably what it looked like.

This feeling of fear and my memory of gas came back to haunt me again a few years later when, still a young child, I was held down in the dentist's chair and a rubber mask was forced over my face as they applied the anaesthetic gas. The fear of gas and dentists remained with me right up until my early twenties when I just decided that enough was enough and somehow managed to overcome it.

My mother and father, Pearl and Harry, were extremely caring parents who gave me all the love and protection anyone could ever wish for. My father told me that, after the Second World War, he and his fellow soldiers wanted to get back to a normal life as quickly as possible and for most of them that simply meant getting a job, getting married and starting a family. My parents married very soon after the war and I was born a year later, becoming part of what would become known as the baby-boom generation. We lived at 68 Dale Valley Road, Oakdale, in an asbestos prefab on one of the hastily erected housing estates that were thrown up to accommodate the enormous number of new families.

I had no concept of whether we were rich or poor: we were just getting by, living an everyday existence. The overriding memory I have of my childhood is one of being happy and being loved, and this above all taught me what really matters in life. It was not until much later that I realised just how poor we had been.

The feeling that you are loved and that someone cares about you is without any doubt the greatest gift on earth.

Material things have no ultimate value and even things you may think are important, such as financial success or social standing, all fade into the distance when compared to the importance of having love in your life. To this day, it remains the bedrock on which I have established my own life and I believe it is ultimately what gave me the ability to sing and to write songs.

I didn't get my first record player until I was about eleven and the first record I owned was 'Diana' by Paul Anka – I'm not sure why. I think it was solely because my mother and I walked into this record shop – we were curious because dedicated record shops had only just started to become popular – and that was the song playing in there at the time. It certainly didn't influence my own future musical direction. The next record I bought was 'Lucille' by Little Richard and that changed everything right then and there ... boom! I think there has been a little bit of Little Richard inside of me ever since.

Most young people have a compelling urge to achieve something with their lives but, for many, the realisation of exactly what form that should take doesn't occur until much later on in life. I count myself as being extremely lucky to have found this 'something' at such an early age. I was even more fortunate to have been able to develop that into what is sometimes laughingly referred to as a 'career'.

At Christmas, when I was twelve, my mother said, 'What do you want as a present?' and I asked if I could have a guitar.

She said, 'No!' We didn't have any money, so I didn't expect it, but come Christmas morning there it was . . . a Rosetti white switch guitar, with a black scratch plate on it. It had an action on it like telegraph wire and it took the strength of Tarzan to push the strings down, but to me it was God.

If my mum and dad had not decided to spend their precious money – over £7 – on buying me a guitar for Christmas, then I am sure my life would have turned out quite differently. I would probably have been tarmacking roads. I was blessed with parents who reacted positively to my enthusiasm for music.

When I was fourteen or fifteen years old, people would often comment about how talented I was, but the simple truth was that I was just plain lucky to have found something I really loved doing at such an early age.

Very shortly after I began playing the guitar at the age of twelve, I wrote the song 'Lucky Man'. I only knew four chords at the time – D, G, A minor and E minor – and I used all of them to compose the song. I don't really know what caused me to think of the title 'Lucky Man' – maybe it was that I was feeling lucky about having my very own guitar or perhaps it was just that moment in a young person's life when you know the time has come to emerge from the chrysalis of childhood and begin a new life as a free-thinking adult. It seems quite strange that time and different perspectives have almost given this song whole new meanings, particularly about the Vietnam War, quite separate from the one I had originally intended.

In the course of my career, I have learned that people have their own impression of what a song means to them, and that's a very good thing: they have their own way of feeling that song, and that's why it's important to them. There is no point banging on about how the song was meant to mean something else. Making music is like giving a gift – it belongs to other people to make of it what they will as soon as it leaves your hands.

Most of my education, such as it was, took place at Henry Harbin Secondary Modern School in Poole. I am not quite sure how the term 'secondary modern' came about but that school was rather aptly named because it wasn't most people's first choice, which was the grammar school (where the smart kids went after the eleven-plus). The number of grammar-school places hadn't been increased to accommodate the baby-boomer generation, so even many clever children ended up at the secondary modern.

One particular occasion at school stands out because it rather typifies the way things were back then. It was the day when the careers officer came around to give the pupils a pep talk about becoming useful members of society and to help them decide what career to choose for their future.

When the talk finally concluded, a questionnaire was handed out that contained a list of fifty or so possible career choices.

The idea was that you should place a number beside three career choices, in order of preference, that you thought might be suitable for you. Needless to say, film director, tennis player, brain surgeon or fashion designer were not listed; the list only featured blue-collar jobs like plumber, electrician, carpenter, mechanic and so on.

Even though I read through the entire list with all the due diligence I could muster, I found nothing that I could possibly envisage doing myself as a career.

At the end of the allotted time, the careers officer collected up all the papers, quickly scanning each one to make sure everyone had filled in at least three choices. When he picked up my paper, he suddenly stopped dead in his tracks and said, 'And what's the matter with you? Why haven't you filled in your three choices?'

I told him that I had honestly tried to find something I wanted to do but that nothing on the list had really appealed to me.

He then said, 'Surely there must be something you like doing?'

'I like playing the guitar,' I replied.

'Playing the guitar is not a job!' he said, mockingly. He then laughingly proclaimed so that the rest of the class could hear, 'Listen to me, Sonny Jim, you had better smarten up your ideas fast or you are going to end up on the scrap heap of life!'

The first feeling I had as he uttered these words was a sense of embarrassment, failure and despair, but when I reflected upon the fact that I had honestly studied the list of jobs and that there was simply no way on God's earth that I was ever going to spend the rest of my life doing any of them, I began to feel a little better.

I realised that rather than simply putting a few meaningless ticks on a page to satisfy some jobsworth careers officer, I'd had the courage of my own convictions. For the first time in my young life, I realised that I was going to make up my own mind about what I wanted to do, and that I was not going to allow anyone to intimidate me.

Luckily, my parents supported me in my desire to think like a free spirit rather than just following the pack.

Soon after I started playing the guitar at the age of twelve, I began taking lessons with my mentor Don Strike, who owned a guitar shop in Westbourne, near Bournemouth. Don taught a number of well-known people including Al Stewart, the Police's Andy Summers, and Robert Fripp, who would later become my great friend and playing partner. Lessons with Don were extremely interesting, at least most of the time.

Prior to teaching guitar, Don was a professional banjo player and some of the techniques he used for that instrument such as cross picking, which helped speed up your playing, featured heavily in his guitar teaching. Robert, Andy and myself were all very influenced by this style of playing and you can hear this reflected in the music of all of our bands that followed. The Police's 'Every Breath You Take',

Robert's solo on King Crimson's '21st Century Schizoid Man' and my own Emerson, Lake & Palmer song 'From the Beginning', for example, all feature cross picking.

Don was a very kind man, but on lesson days he would stand no messing around. Each week he would give me a sheet of music to learn and when I came back the following week, I would have to play it back to him. The problem was that it was usually stuff like 'Blue Moon' or 'Red Sails in the Sunset', but when I got home, I just wanted to play Chuck Berry and Hank Marvin – rock and roll. So, the day before the class, I would just try and learn Don's chosen song as quickly as I could by ear. When it came to playing it for him, I would usually get to a point where I didn't get it quite right and he would know I hadn't been following the dots on the sheet. He had a particularly effective remedy for slackers or for anyone not following the dots properly. This consisted of a sharp whack across the fingers of the left hand with the wooden ruler he used for conducting and keeping time. One or two of those and you would soon be right back on track, I can promise you. Don's lessons were a true musical revelation, though, and those days we spent together were incredibly valuable for the rest of my life.

Don had his own philosophy about performing and I will never forget him sitting me down during one of my final lessons with him and saying to me, 'Okay, now listen, son, I want you to understand something: whenever it comes to performing it is always four for them and one for you!'

I honestly had no idea what he was talking about and, with a rather vacant look on my face, I sheepishly asked him what he meant. He looked back at me with a really stern look in his eyes and said, 'Look, it's your job as a musician to entertain the audience. They haven't paid their hard-earned money to come and watch you entertain yourself. For every four songs you play and that you are sure they like, you are allowed to play just one for yourself which you like even if they don't, so it's four for them and one for you.'

I have always remembered Don's words of wisdom and can tell you that, after forty or fifty years of playing concerts, this balance is not far wrong.

Don Strike was a wonderful chap; he was an extremely conscientious teacher who took an extraordinary pride in all of his students and I consider myself very privileged indeed to have had the good fortune to have been taught by him.

I worked with Don for about two and a half years before deciding to follow my own creative path as a guitar player. The pull of rock-and-roll music proved to be so powerful I just couldn't justify spending any more time learning formal guitar exercises or absorbing any more of Don's crafty chord inversions. Now, of course, I wish I had, as it is not every day that you come across someone who is willing to offer you something that took them a lifetime to acquire.

■ ■ ■

During the very early days of being taught by Don, I formed a little band with two of my friends from school. We would go along to family parties and small local bingo halls and play a repertoire consisting of songs from the pop charts and some of the pieces I had learned during my guitar lessons.

Although we must have been pretty dreadful, people were still so kind, applauding enthusiastically after every song. That early encouragement was incredibly important.

One thing I discovered while playing at family parties was that I could earn money by doing the thing I loved. I made my first little bit of cash by challenging the guests to name any song from the charts and, if I could play it, they paid me sixpence, and if I couldn't then of course I paid them the same amount. My repertoire of chart hits stood at somewhere around 220 songs. The problem was that after a while they began to wise up and became fed up of handing over the money. Still, it was great while it lasted!

From the age of twelve onwards, I would sometimes go to the local youth club or dance halls. The Teddy boys were the kings of fashion at the time: velvet collars, crepe-soled shoes, Elvis sideboards and a cowboy string necktie. The music was strictly 1950s rock and roll, with songs by Bill Haley, Ricky Nelson, Jerry Lee Lewis, Little Richard and so on.

The bands that played in these venues invariably wore brightly coloured, matching sparkle jackets or alternatively leather motorcycle jackets and Levi's, and you could always bank on some sort of a fight breaking out before the end of the night due to the atmosphere always being tinged with hostility. The catalyst was a combination of the teenage girls wanting to try out the effectiveness of their newly acquired attributes and the boys responding with a macho display of violence – a ritual that has probably existed since time began.

On one occasion, when I was fourteen or fifteen, I went further afield to a glitzy ballroom in Boscombe, a small town very close to Bournemouth and quite near to where I grew up. I went there to watch a 'professional' band, whose name I am ashamed to say now escapes me, that had come all the way down from London that night to perform.

From the word go it was obvious that they were in a completely different league to the local bands I had seen previously. I will never forget standing there being absolutely awestruck as the lead guitarist and rhythm guitarist strode on to the stage carrying their two matching Fiesta Red Fender Jaguars followed closely by the bass player carrying his matching Fiesta Red Fender Precision Bass. They looked terrific in their matching black Savile Row suits and they sounded great as well.

The glitter ball hanging high up in the ceiling began to spin as they struck up the first few chords and the girls below started screaming as the whole place erupted into a whirlwind of frenzied excitement. It was then, in the midst of all this rock-and-roll chaos, that everything seemed to fall into place.

Although I could see that the band were extremely professional, the fact was that after having had a couple of years of lessons from Don, I realised that I could play the guitar as well if not better than any of the professionals up on that stage. My destiny was cast.

I could see that with the right equipment and enough hard work, it just might be possible for me to have that same thrilling effect upon an audience, and perhaps one day even become a professional musician myself.

That night when I went back home I was completely unable to sleep. Again and again I could hear the sound of those Fender guitars playing round and round in my head.

A few days later, I heard the same unmistakable sound of a Fender guitar playing once again, but this time coming from a tiny little Dansette record player blasting away on a bare wooden decorator's table stood in the corner of the local youth club dance hall near where I lived.

I immediately went up and asked the DJ what the record was. The answer that came back set me on a path that changed the course of my life as a guitar player. The tune was 'Apache', recorded by the Shadows, and the guitarist's name was Hank B. Marvin.

Hank played a Fiesta Red Fender Stratocaster rather than a Jaguar but they are just like children from the same family: although there are some fundamental differences, those two guitars are unmistakably related to each other and you cannot fail to hear this reflected in the sound they make.

Hank was not only an inspiration for me, but for almost all of the great guitar players who followed after him: Jimi Hendrix, Mark Knopfler, Gary Moore, Ritchie Blackmore, Jeff Beck, Brian May – actually the list is endless. Most, if not all, of these players have openly acknowledged the influence and inspiration that Hank's guitar-playing had upon them. It was not so much Hank's speed, although he is a really good technical player, but his sound and soulful use of melody that captivated everybody.

Many years later, I met up with Hank in Brian Bennett's studio. Brian was the drummer with the Shadows and Hank was there overdubbing some orchestral recordings of the band's music.

The moment I entered through the door Hank smiled and shook my hand as if I were some long-lost friend.

'Fancy a cup of tea?' he said.

I nodded and smiled as he disappeared back through the control-room door.

A few minutes later he returned with a tray of tea and biscuits that he had prepared himself. I thought then: what a lovely way to greet someone and put them so completely at ease. It said a lot about Hank and why he is so loved and respected by his millions of fans.

After we had sat down, I explained to Hank that the reason I had come to see him was that I just wanted to thank him for being such a wonderful inspiration, and that he helped me to develop the vision for my career. He smiled and told me that he was actually a big fan of my own music with King Crimson and Emerson, Lake & Palmer, and thought that it was great that we could meet up together after all these years.

A little later on, I asked him how it was that he managed to achieve his very special sound and explained to him how, as young guitar players, we all went to extraordinary lengths to try and copy it. We all bought the same Fender guitar and the same Vox AC30 amplifier, we all used the same Binson echo chamber and studied the tunes he had written note for note, but no matter how hard we tried, none of us could ever get the sound exactly right.

At first, being the extremely humble person he is, Hank looked slightly bewildered and a little embarrassed. After a few moments, though, he turned and said, 'Well, I suppose if I do have any sort of special sound, it is most probably due to the fact that when I first began playing, I held the pick totally the wrong way round.'

He then proceeded to demonstrate this by holding a plectrum in the same way that you hold a pen. We both fell about laughing because it is far easier to hold the thing the right way than it is the wrong way.

Apparently, young Hank continued using this wrong grip until one day when a friend who also played the guitar came up to him and pointed out the error of his ways. Hank said that he felt quite embarrassed at the time and from then on was determined to get it right. He explained that despite years of practising with the right technique, his grip never really became orthodox or normal, and in fact had ended up being a sort of halfway house. 'That's all I can put it down to,' he said, as he handed over his original Stratocaster for me to play.

Unless you play the guitar, it is hard for me to explain to you how it felt holding the very guitar that shone the light of inspiration on my whole musical career, but suffice to say that it was a very special moment for me and one I will never forget.

During my meeting with Hank, I believe that I did find out what it was that made him sound so great. It was not the equipment, or even the way he held his pick. It was the spirit and the soul of the man himself.

Hank is extremely humble and gentle in his approach, but at the same time he is a very deep, spiritual person, and you cannot help but feel that he has some kind of inner strength and calm control. Somehow you get the feeling that, for him, everything is almost effortless. I am sure he would laugh at these words as, of course, life is not easy for anyone and no doubt he practised endlessly to became the great guitarist that we all know, but that is the impression I came away with.

Both as a person and as a guitar player, Hank is a star of the very finest calibre and all of us who play the instrument owe him a great deal. I still find it a rather strange phenomenon that Hank and the Shadows are so little known in the United States. I think many people there would be extremely surprised to discover just how big an influence he was upon so many of their all-time guitar-playing idols.

OPENING NOTES

So, it was Hank who ignited my vision of becoming a professional musician and it was Don Strike who taught me how
to do it. I owe them both a huge debt of gratitude.

CHAPTER 2

The Early Bands

Some of my memories regarding my early bands in the mid-1960s have now begun to merge into a bit of a blur, but I do remember travelling around in these old converted vans in what seemed to be like one long never-ending journey back and forth across England, sleeping in the van at night and always feeling cold and often hungry as well.

During those early years, the van was an extremely important part of the set-up. Not only was it our means of transport, but it was also the place where we ate, slept, talked and took care of pretty much everything else that life entailed.

I would estimate that somewhere around 90 per cent of our lives at that time were spent living or travelling in the van. It was something like being on board a pirate ship, where even though there was a certain sense of romanticism, freedom and adventure, it was nevertheless quite a miserable and hard way to live, and at times extremely dangerous. I was involved in at least five or six fairly serious collisions during those early years, most of which were sadly due to the fact that we would often drive all through the night and on into the next morning in order to avoid spending yet another cold night sleeping in some desolate, rain-soaked car park.

The technique we used for driving through the night was the sort of thing you might see in a cartoon but we really did it: in order to help the driver to keep his eyes open, we would break a couple of matchsticks in half and rest the broken end just below the eye on top of the cheek (to provide the required grip), and then have the smooth end wedged firmly underneath the eyelid itself. This, of course, was a very silly thing to do, but it always caused a lot of laughter and that, if nothing else, helped whoever was driving to stay awake.

Vans were so important back then that they were often used almost like a currency. For example, you would regularly see musicians placing adverts in the local newspaper, looking for a 'job in a band', and the advert would read something like, 'Drummer looking for band, has own equipment plus own van', in the hope that the van would act as some sort of added incentive to be chosen for the gig.

My first real 'semi-pro' band was Unit 4 (not to be confused with Unit 4 + 2, which had a big hit with 'Concrete and Clay' in 1965). Unit 4 was quite a good little band that I formed together with some of the local boys from near where I lived in Poole. Throughout 1965, we would travel around in an old converted ambulance to play shows all over the south coast of England. The ambulance turned out to be particularly useful whenever we encountered long traffic jams or queues as the emergency bell was still working.

One enduring memory I have of Unit 4 is playing the Lagland Street Boys' Club in Poole. Our repertoire consisted mainly of material from the charts, which of course included many of the early Beatles songs, the Shadows, Motown and so on. We had started to become quite popular by the time we played the club and when we walked on to the stage we were absolutely deafened by all the girls screaming. After the show had finished, we went outside to discover that the girls had obliterated the windows of the van by covering them in messages and phone numbers written in red and pink lipstick. Needless to say, for young boys of sixteen and seventeen years old, this was a truly heart-warming sight.

Unit 4 often played at a local pub called the Oakdale, very near to where I used to live. Every Saturday night, just as in Elton's song, it would be exactly the same routine. We would play right up until the bell sounded for last orders, and then, as if it were by some pre-ordained signal, fighting would break out. Chairs and bottles would begin to fly across the bar as all the non-combatants scurried around, bent over double, trying to avoid the hurled debris as they headed for the door.

The problem for us was that, in the middle of all this mayhem, we still had to load out our equipment. In the end, we devised a clever little plan whereby my father would go outside and wait until the bell sounded and then, as soon as the fighting broke out, we would quickly hand the guitars and amps out through an open window conveniently located right behind the stage.

Another venue where we would regularly perform was in the Cellar Club, Poole's equivalent of Liverpool's famous Cavern Club. When Robert Fripp was a young boy at college with little or no money, he would climb over the wall of the Cellar Club to come and watch me play. We had often sometimes run through lessons together at his house when we were both being taught guitar by Don Strike. In fact, sometimes when I was playing in Unit 4, Robert – who did not have his own band at the time – used to come up on stage and we would play a song together, 'Malagueña', which Don had made us learn.

Every time we played at the Cellar Club, the place was so packed the sweat would literally run down from the walls in streams, and in the summer the temperature almost became unbearable with people often fainting or passing out through heat exhaustion. It is remarkable that we were able to perform at all in these conditions, but perform we did and often for three or four hours at a stretch.

After Unit 4, I was in a band called the Time Checks in 1966, and later on I had a short stint in the Shy Limbs, but the other early band that really stands out in my memory is the Shame. This was the first band I had formed that had real attitude. Apart from myself, the band consisted of the late

Malcolm Brasher on bass, Billy Nims on drums and Jon Petterssen on rhythm guitar, and later John Dickerson joined on keyboards. The Shame were not together for very long but there was something about the personalities of the people in the band that still keeps its spirit alive in my memory to this day.

That's not to say that we did not have some tough times on the road. We were often short of money, so we had our own version of a chip butty where we would eat out the middle of a loaf, pack the hole with chips and then eat the whole lot. When we were playing up in Carlisle, I caught pneumonia. We had slept in the van during a freezing night – it was like sleeping in a metal icebox – and when I awoke I was blue. We had to drive 300 miles home and, when we finally got there, I just collapsed and passed out. My mother called the doctor and I was given oxygen and put on penicillin.

The Shame was the first band that I was in to have proper London-based management, Harvey Block Associates (Dru Harvey and Derek Block), who also managed the Walker Brothers. The move to London was always seen as being absolutely crucial as it was the centre of the recording industry and the place where all the major studios were located. Signing up with Dru Harvey was at least a step in the right direction, even if we were still based on the south coast.

I was already a great admirer of Jimi Hendrix, and 'Hey Joe' was a regular feature of our set list. Dru Harvey managed to get us on as the support band for headliners Jimi Hendrix and Ten Years After at a gig at Sussex University. We also played the famous Speakeasy in London in support of Procol Harum.

It was around then that my recording career began when the Shame cut a Janis Ian song called 'Don't Go Away Little Girl', which came out on Poppy Records, a subsidiary of RCA, in 1967. The song was slightly Beatles-like and a bit psychedelic – very 1967 – but it was a decent track. We cut the record in Pye's studios at Marble Arch in London. Even though it never became a big hit – it was apparently banned by the BBC because the advert for the single had a picture of me with a crown of thorns and a halo – for me the whole experience was a huge revelation and an insight into the world of recording and making records.

With the cutting of this record, my career as a musician had changed from one of being purely a performer to one of being a recording artist as well; perhaps the most important transition any professional musician can make.

After the release of 'Don't Go Away Little Girl', the Shame had a stab at making a couple more recordings, but these really didn't amount to much and eventually the band disintegrated when Malcolm and Billy went back to resume their former careers at art college.

Before long, I received a call from manager Dru Harvey, who told me that he was now looking after a band called the Gods and asked if I would be interested in joining. The Gods were one of those bands that were a bit like a musical roundabout, where it seemed that everyone who was anyone had been associated with them at one time or another. Mick Taylor was a member in his early years before joining the Rolling Stones in 1969, but we didn't overlap. Ken Hensley and Lee Kerslake who later joined Uriah Heep were in the band – I knew Lee from when he was drumming in a local band in Bournemouth – but I didn't really connect with anyone musically.

Nonetheless, here was an offer to join a professional band from London and for me at the time it was definitely a step in the right direction, so I really didn't need much persuading. It was also very exciting because it was the first time that I had moved away from my parents and set out to live on my own or, actually in this case, with five other members of the Gods in a rundown flat in Chiswick in south-west London.

I particularly remember the day in 1968 when I left my parents' house in Poole because, even though my mother was quite used to having me travel around the country, she knew that this time it was different: I would not be returning, at least not for a while, and I saw the tears in her eyes as I waved goodbye.

The London flat that was about to become my home was a far cry from our family house in Poole. I parked outside this big old Victorian house in Chiswick and walked up the stone stairs to the front door, and was bewildered by the sight of row after row of little white doorbells all with paper names stuck inside them. 'Surely all these different people can't be living in this one house?' I thought.

Well, that was the first little clue I got regarding what I was about to walk into. Eventually, Lee came to the door and welcomed me in.

I walked down this long and rather dilapidated corridor and entered a large room right at the end. It was one of those large, old-style Victorian drawing rooms with a very high ceiling, save for the fact that this particular room had been divided up with hardboard walls to create four separate compartments.

There was no heating in the flat but each compartment had its own electric light bulb overhead that could also be adapted to plug in a small electric fire. You could either have the light on or the heating but not both, otherwise the fuses throughout the whole house would blow.

Weary from travelling and all the excitement of moving in to the new flat, I decided to retire to my little compartment and lie down on the mattress that was on the floor. After sleeping in the back of a van for so long, even this spartan set-up looked quite appealing to me – although it soon became obvious that it was a breeding ground for cockroaches. In any case, as things turned out it would not be too long before we all moved out into a far more comfortable house in nearby Dukes Avenue.

The Gods had a road manager called Lil (I never did find out his real name) who was also a guitar player and his overriding passion was for the blues. I will always remember walking in to the flat one day and seeing him kneeling on the floor playing his Fender Telecaster guitar, with his head stuck through a hole that had been cut out of the side of a very large cardboard box. Apparently, there was a Vox AC30 amplifier inside the box, a combination he always swore gave him the authentic sound of the blues. I simply took his word for it and said no more.

Lil was sweet and long-suffering, and his passion and enthusiasm for the music he loved, in his case the blues, was something that I always felt was missing from the Gods.

The concept behind the Gods always seemed to me to be more of a business arrangement than being a real band. We used to travel all over the country playing small gigs in local theatres and so on, but we never really developed any particular style or musical identity.

That is not to say that we did not have an amusing time, such as on the day we all went down to Carnaby Street in London to buy matching stage clothes. As well as playing keyboards, Ken Hensley looked after the band's financial affairs at the time and he had struck up an arrangement with some entrepreneurial clothes baron cum fashion designer in Carnaby Street who thought it would be a good idea to dress us all in brightly coloured, frilly satin glam-rock shirts with matching satin pants. I shudder now to think what we must have looked like. As a matter of fact, I do believe that somewhere there still exists an old poster of the Gods dressed in these stomach-churning shirts.

I was only with the Gods for maybe six or eight months

and left before we ever got to make any recordings together. I honestly can't remember how it all came to an end, but I never really felt comfortable in the band. Perhaps this had something to do with the fact that I had been more or less ushered in to fill a void rather than forming a band with people I respected musically, as I had always done in the past. Being in the Gods had taught me the key to forming a great band: you simply have to respect the people you are working with and they need to respect you, because the moment this respect fails or is taken for granted, the whole structure just comes tumbling down.

CHAPTER 3

Court in Session

I received a call from Robert Fripp soon after I moved back to Dorset in 1968. To earn some money, I was working at Aish Technologies in Poole, and I was trying to figure out what my next move would be – I had enjoyed a taste of working as a professional musician but in the end it looked like it had all come to nothing.

Robert asked if I would like to be the lead singer for his new band. We had become close when we spent all that time practising together for Don Strike's guitar lessons – and I knew he was a really good player – so the idea appealed to me immediately.

His band was originally called Giles, Giles and Fripp and featured the brothers Michael and Peter Giles, who respectively played drums and bass and shared the singing duties, and Ian McDonald, who had just joined the band to play saxophone, clarinet and flute. They were signed to Decca Records but had just been told that unless they hired a proper lead singer and became commercially relevant, they would be dropped from the label. Around this time, Peter Giles left the band. During the call, I told Robert not to worry and assured him that, together, we could easily get things going in the right direction.

There was a brief silence on the phone. Then Robert said, in a slightly nervous tone and with a strong Dorset accent: 'Gregory' – he always used my full name when he wanted to persuade me to do something – 'I wonder if as well as being the lead singer, you could possibly consider playing the bass instead of electric guitar?'

'Why bass?' I asked.

'Well', he said, 'I'm already playing electric guitar and we don't really need two guitarists, but if you played bass then we could keep the band down to being a four-piece.'

I thought about it for a moment. *Four strings instead of six. How hard can it be?* Plus they already had a record deal. 'Okay,' I said, 'don't worry, I'll take care of it.'

Little did I know at that moment, but switching from guitar to bass would be a difficult transition to make. And I was about to be made acutely aware of this.

Robert changed the name of the band to King Crimson and I returned to London. Our first rehearsal took place in the front room of a small house in Kilburn where Giles, Giles and Fripp had been living. I went along with my newly acquired

Fender Jazz bass and met Michael and Ian. Then I plugged in to some grubby old Marshall amplifier they had rented for me to play through.

After the first ten or twelve bars, Michael began to hit the snare drum hard and repeatedly in order to stop everyone playing. He slowly lifted his eyes towards me with a look of pity and mild resignation, and began politely to explain that the bass *never, never, ever, ever* plays on the off-beat when the snare drum is playing.

I must have looked to him like a rabbit caught in the headlights because I honestly had no idea what on earth he was talking about. He went on to explain one of the most fundamental and basic rules of bass playing: in order for the snare drum to cut through and give the music a powerful off-beat feel, there has to be a brief moment of silence as the snare beat falls and the bass is not playing. Otherwise there is no clarity and the sound is mushed. I felt dreadfully embarrassed. It sounded so obvious once Michael had spelled it out. However, this one little moment of education opened up a new world of awareness for me. The rest of the rehearsal went well and everyone was happy with my voice and our new line-up.

Michael proved to be a great drummer. He could play different time signatures with each hand and each foot simultaneously and then come back in on time.

I felt like I was in a band with proper, skilful musicians, and it was a bit of a step up from just being in a band because you could get the girls and the attention – King Crimson were trying to do something new with their music, and wanted to deliver it with care and subtlety as well as passion. I was something of a raw recruit, and I had to learn fast. I soon developed my own way of playing the bass. I used a guitar pick, rather than playing with my fingers, which meant that I could play fast. I was trying to develop a sound a little like the one you can get out of the bottom end of a Steinway.

A few days after our first rehearsal, Ian invited us round to a flat in West Kensington to meet a friend of his called Pete Sinfield. When I went to Pete's flat for the first time, I noticed how thoughtfully it had been decorated with Moroccan pillows featuring little mirrors and Indian rugs, which he had hanging on the walls. The exotic atmosphere was accentuated by the smell of burning incense in the air, which blended with the hash that a number of us smoked at the time. (Neither Robert nor Michael smoked hash but they both used to roll their own cigarettes using Old Holborn, the pungent tobacco. I can still hear Michael's voice explaining to me that putting a piece of orange peel in a tin of tobacco always helped to keep it fresh.)

It was around that time in London that music was beginning to move away from the conventional three-minute pop song and towards conceptual albums – with hugely influential and inspiring albums such as *Electric Ladyland* by Jimi Hendrix and *Sgt. Pepper's Lonely Hearts Club Band* by the Beatles. Ian and Pete mentioned that they too had written a conceptual song, which they wanted try it out with the band. It was called 'The Court of the Crimson King'.

Robert and I decided to move into a flat together in a large Victorian house in Leinster Square in Bayswater, west London. Neither of us were domesticated and it quickly became like the flat in the film *Withnail and I*. No one dared venture into the kitchen for fear of being attacked by the sink monsters that lurked in the pile of unwashed dishes.

Leinster Square was only a couple of blocks from Portobello Road, where we would often go to hear the latest music being played in the 'head shops'. These were little hole-in-the-wall operations that sold the latest cool music releases and also supplied drug paraphernalia such as rolling machines, cigarette papers and hash pipes. They were a one-stop shop for hippies.

Robert would ask me for advice about how the band should look on stage so we would go to down to the Portobello antiques shops and junk stalls for inspiration. Unlike Robert, I had been in a number of different bands previously and had learned a bit about stagecraft, experimented with clobber and got a bit of a stage look. Robert was still wearing the maroon V-neck pullover and plaid shirt he had been wearing since college.

We tried out various styles for him back at our flat but it was no good dressing him up in frilly shirts, which were the fashion at the time, or anything like that. Then I remembered that he had always been intrigued by the violinist Niccolò Paganini, who looked like a Satan worshipper. He would stand between two black candles and play the most difficult violin pieces imaginable at extraordinary speeds. Then he would challenge other violinists to public duels to see who could play the fastest. He would even taunt his rivals by ripping off two strings from his violin and playing the piece in exactly the same way and at the same pace. No one could match him.

I suggested to Robert that we could perhaps build up something around the black magic image of Paganini and maybe dress him in a cloak or something dark and austere. Robert loved the idea, so off we went down Portobello Road again to visit the antique shops and junk stalls. The first thing we saw was a black top hat. Perfect – just the thing. Next we found a black cape, black shirt and black shoes. The look was complete. Robert's rather strange stage persona began to develop out of that look. Later on came all the other antics such as him playing with his back to the audience or hidden behind the speakers.

That evening, I went to the Marquee Club in Soho to watch a band called Spooky Tooth. When I returned home to Leinster Square, I pressed the light switch but the lights didn't come on. Sometimes the bulbs blew and everyone in the building was too lazy to change them so I just accepted it and walked up the stairs in the dark. I noticed that there was a dim light flickering at the top of the staircase. As I drew a little closer, I suddenly saw this horrific white face complete with crooked teeth and a black top hat. The face belonged to a stooped figure, which was standing there dressed in a black cloak like Jack the Ripper and holding a candle up to its face. The face was glaring at me with menacing intent. My heart nearly stopped.

'You bastard!' I shouted.

Yes, after pulling the light bulb out of its socket, Robert had sat up all night, wearing that costume and a set of false teeth, waiting for me to come home just so that he could scare the shit out of me. It must have taken the best part of ten minutes for me to calm down. I'm sure it gave Robert an immense amount of pleasure.

In the early weeks of King Crimson, we met up with David Enthoven and John Gaydon of E.G. Management and they soon started to look after the band. David and John were both former public school boys. John had gone to Eton and David had attended Harrow, where he had struck up a friendship with Chris Blackwell of Island Records. We had cut ties with Decca and Chris was interested in signing us. We were taken to see him and knew straight away that Chris was different from most label heads. He had a strange and wonderful work ethic. When we went to any other record company, we would be taken to the president's office and have to sit awkwardly on old leather-clad seats. Chris never even had his own office. He sat with all the staff, usually perching on someone's desk.

King Crimson were looking for a record deal that would allow us to make an album in the way that we had envisioned, without interference or compromise.

'We want to make the record we want to make, not the one *you* want us to make,' we told Chris.

Incredibly, Chris insisted that he wouldn't have it any other way. So we signed the deal with Island and prepared to make our first record.

The early rehearsals for the album took place in a basement underneath a little Greek café on the Fulham Palace Road. We were an unusual group of people, with a strange blend of different personalities, and none of us seemed to want to follow the rules. I realised quite early on that the result of this was that we could make music that was dangerous, innovative and passionate.

At first, we discussed using a producer and, because our reputation had spread so quickly, our name came to the attention of the Moody Blues' producer Tony Clarke. Tony arranged to come down and meet the band and listen to the music. When he arrived, he rang the doorbell to the basement and our road manager Dick Frazer went up to let him in. As he walked down the stairs we noticed that behind him were four or five other people. They were the Moody Blues.

We played them '21st Century Schizoid Man' and 'The Court of the Crimson King'. I could immediately see by the reaction on their faces that they were shocked. I think they had come expecting to hear a modified version of their own light, orchestral style. They were not ready for the passion of the vocals or the speed of Robert's guitar-playing or the intensity of our band in general. We rounded off their visit with 'Mars, the Bringer of War' from Holst's *The Planets*. They left quietly.

We moved to Wessex Studios to record the album. We took Tony with us and started work but we quickly came to realise that working with a producer was not giving us the freedom we needed. So, we decided to go it alone. During the rest of the recording sessions everything happened fast and our ideas were often spontaneous rather than preconceived. There were few discussions or deliberations or retakes because we all pretty much sensed what we had to do. It all just flowed naturally without us forcing ideas on each other. As Ian McDonald once said, there was a shared musical intent about the band.

Being part of King Crimson in those formative days really felt like we were 'following wind'. Everything just happened without effort. It was bizarre. The album *In the Court of the Crimson King* not only captured a moment in time but it also spoke of a new awareness, a dream that shone a light into the future. It announced the arrival of a new generation.

Towards the end of the sessions, we started to discuss the album cover. We wanted the full package — gatefold sleeves, striking artwork, in-depth credits — and Pete Sinfield mentioned that he had a friend called Barry Godber who was a graphic artist. We agreed to let Barry have a try.

A few days later we had just finished a take for the record-ing of '21st Century Schizoid Man' and I saw someone walk into the studio with a large sheet of cardboard wrapped up in brown paper and tied with string. I didn't know who he was until Pete explained that it was Barry, and that he had come to show us his ideas for the album cover. Bands are always sceptical about album covers so I was expecting to hear at least one person say, 'Oh no, I can't live with that.'

Barry took a pair of scissors out of his pocket, snipped the string and tore off the paper, making sure we couldn't see the picture. Then he flipped it over and dropped it on the floor. We looked down and there was the screaming face of schizoid man! How could he have known? We were in shock. If ever there was a picture that could evoke the screaming, raw, wild feeling of '21st Century Schizoid Man', it was this one. Everyone knew that this was the album cover. There was no discussion.

The strangest part about this story – and most tragic – is that only a short time later Barry Godber fell down dead in the street from a heart attack. He was only twenty-one years old. I can never quite separate in my own mind the image that he created and the terrible fate that awaited him so soon after it was delivered to us.

The image was a tribute to Barry's talent as an artist and absolutely befitting a recording that has now gone on to become a classic of its era. It's possibly the best record I ever made.

■ ■ ■

Right from the first King Crimson show, it was obvious that the band was special. It wasn't just that we went down well. The audiences were shocked when we performed. We opened with '21st Century Schizoid Man' and halfway through the song we put the venue into complete darkness and then used a strobe-lighting effect during the blindingly fast guitar solo passage, which was extremely disorientating. This was further intensified by Robert glaring at the audience with a fixed stare, later referred to as 'the death look', and my distorted singing. It was not uncommon to see people cowering as if the stage was about to roll over them. And that was only the first song! And if you had taken a few of the wrong pills, believe me . . . you would want out of there.

The shows often ended with Holst's 'Mars, the Bringer of War'. It is one of the most intimidating pieces of music ever written and, although we were only a four-piece band, we played it with all the menace we could muster. Part of the magic of King Crimson, though, was its ability to switch dynamics. One moment it was the brutal onslaught of '21st Century Schizoid Man', the next the audience was gently caressed by the velvet sound of Ian's flute-playing in 'I Talk to the Wind'; the power of 'Epitaph' contrasted with the more wistful, folky 'Moonchild', and I would modulate my voice according to the nature of each song. Another element that seemed to be distinctly different about King Crimson was that we all placed as much importance upon listening to each other play as we did upon playing our own instruments, and this made the music take place very much in the moment rather than always being preconceived.

Our show was surreal in a way, but there was a streak of dark reality too. Our lyrics could be political – Pete's lyrics to 'Schizoid Man' included 'Politicians' funeral pyre / innocence raped with napalm fire' and directly referenced what was happening in Vietnam – and we tried to tackle big themes such as injustice and suffering. If there ever was a record that deserved the word 'progressive', it was *In the Court of the Crimson King* because it looked forward, it was new – although I don't like the word 'progressive' because of how it has been adopted to pigeonhole the music. It sounds elitist and pretentious. We simply wanted to be original and to make art rather than commercial rubbish. We wanted our songs to mean something, but that didn't mean we were high-minded and thought we were superior to everyone else.

When we started playing the songs live, before the album was released, we were already starting to take off but we didn't expect the album to be a hit. The record was released in October 1969 and, to our surprise, reached number five in the UK album charts.

One of my most vivid memories of the early shows by King Crimson was when we performed at the legendary Marquee Club in Wardour Street in Soho. The Marquee was famous for being the place where new talent got discovered and it was also a proving ground for more established acts searching for recognition. If you went down well at the Marquee, you were almost certainly on the road to success.

I doubt if there is one single famous British band from that era that didn't perform there. Everyone from the Rolling Stones to Jimi Hendrix, the Yardbirds, the Who, Rod Stewart, Jethro Tull, Led Zeppelin . . . the list just goes on and on.

Expectations were high the night King Crimson played at the Marquee. *Could they be as good as people say?* We were determined not to disappoint. I peered out from behind the stage and, although I have since performed in front of far larger audiences, my memory of that sight of the crowd that night still gives me a thrill. The Marquee had vastly oversold the show and the crowd was way beyond the official capacity – so much so that the audience were literally climbing the walls. When we eventually came on to the stage there was a deafening roar of anticipation as if an epic Roman games was about to begin. And we didn't disappoint. In that one night, the band were hoisted into a different league.

We quickly gained a reputation in and around London. From gatherings of sixty people at our first gigs, we went on to be headliners a few weeks later and, without any publicity whatsoever, we were playing to audiences of five hundred. Word was spreading fast within the music business as well. One night we were playing at the Revolution club in London and I looked out at the crowd and saw Jimi Hendrix staring back at me. He had come to the show to check *us* out.

Within six months of our first gig, we were performing with the Rolling Stones at Hyde Park in London on 5 July 1969 to an audience of over a quarter of a million people. According to some reports, over twice that number were there. I had never seen that many people, even in a film. It was an unreal spectacle. The park was so thick with people you couldn't see the grass anywhere. You could barely see the trees because so many people had clambered on to the branches. It felt beautiful, too, because the spirit of the age was one of goodwill and peace. It was about sharing love and awareness. This was even the feeling down the front among the Hell's Angels, doing the shoulder dance or whatever it is they do. And next to them were the flower people. It was bizarre.

We were first on. We played our set and at the end we got a standing ovation from the entire crowd. That was it. We were really on our way now: *250,000 people can't be wrong*, we thought. Thank goodness we had our managers to keep us in check. They made sure we kept paying our dues, learning our craft as a band and never deluding ourselves that we would go straight to Madison Square Garden. So, after Hyde Park, we went back to playing the clubs.

CHAPTER 4

Crimson America

Not long after the Hyde Park show, the buzz about King Crimson reached the United States. We were offered a tour there and flew over to John F. Kennedy International Airport in New York. We were greeted in arrivals by a portly Italian gentleman with grey-white hair and a white beard, and a sunshine smile with suntan to match.

This was our new American manager. The legendary Dee Anthony.

He was simply a tidal wave of enthusiasm and positivity; something that English people at that time had little understanding about. As we walked out of the airport, I was struck by the sight of a long row of bright yellow New York taxis and two enormous black Cadillac Fleetwood stretch limousines. At last, here I was, in the United States of America.

Manny, one of the limo drivers, jumped out and opened the door with a stylish flourish, beckoning us to step inside. Of course, we had only seen cars like these in the movies and for us the ride into the city was like a dream. During the journey, the radio came on and Dee, who was sitting in the front, suddenly turned around and said, 'Listen!'

The radio station was playing 'The Court of the Crimson King'. Halfway through the song, Manny reached back and handed us a lit joint and, with a deep voice reminiscent of Barry White, said: 'Welcome to the Big Apple.'

We drove across Brooklyn Bridge in the Fleetwood Cadillac and saw the Manhattan skyline for the first time. *There it is!* It was just breathtaking. And *In the Court of the Crimson King* was playing on the radio. It turned out that Dee had bribed the DJ to play the record just as we crossed the Brooklyn Bridge. He had it timed so perfectly. That was Dee. He was a showman.

Meeting someone as charismatic as Dee was part and parcel of all the new experiences we were having. Even booking into the hotel in New York was exciting. To be honest, I hadn't stayed in that many hotels with elevators until then. I was amazed by the buttons lighting up in the lift – there were fifty floors! And I remember touching the buttons again and again just to see them light up. Then I stood by the window in my room, looking down at Manhattan for a long, long time, marvelling that I had made it to America. Now we had to make it *in* America.

As far as Dee was concerned, the band was already a hit even before we got off the plane. All we had to do was follow his plan and all would be well. We had no concept about the actual size of the United States or what achieving success there really meant, but such was the power of Dee's enthusiasm that anyone who encountered it would be carried along and so it was with us. He took great pleasure in making things happen that most people would consider impossible. He was partly a Svengali manager like Elvis's Colonel Tom Parker, and he was partly a fan. He would stand on the side of the stage all night and after every song he would be cheering. He was so passionate.

He was smooth, too, wherever we went, and would tip the doormen at the front of hotels in order to ensure that they were focused on getting things done for him. He showed me his technique one day. He concealed a $20 bill (Dee always referred to it as a 'twenty spot') in the palm of his right hand and then, when he stepped out of the car, he would immediately shake hands with the doorman. Of course, the doorman instantly felt the note pressing into the palm of his hand and, in that one small moment, a secret little bond was established without a word needing to be spoken. The doorman's dignity was preserved and, once he had glanced down at the denomination, he was totally onside.

'Certainly, Mr Anthony, I'll take care of everything for you. Please let me take you right to the front desk.'

Bada bing! Bada boom! as Dee would often say.

Dee was born Anthony D'Addario and grew up in the Bronx in the 1940s, and he went on to manage a number of artists including Tony Bennett. He told me that over the years – simply due to being an Italian in the music business – he had met a number of the well-known Italian crime bosses, who would often say hello to him in a restaurant or on the street. One night Dee took us to dinner at one of his favourite Italian restaurants down in Little Italy. As we all entered the restaurant and stood in the lobby, Dee began talking to the maître d' about our table when suddenly he turned round and ushered us all back out on to the pavement. He had seen someone who had mob connections sitting in the corner of the restaurant. Although he had no problems with the old gangsters on a personal level, and made sure that he was polite and respectful, he tried to avoid becoming too friendly because there was the risk they could suddenly assign him a dubious role which he would be unable refuse.

'"No" is just not a word they understand,' he told me, with a huge smile on his face.

Just now and again, you come across someone who is truly luminous and Dee was one of those rare people who lit up a room simply by his presence. Dee passed away in 2009 and, to me, it was more than simply the loss of a great human being and a great manager, it was truly the end of an era.

■ ■ ■

In the euphoric early days after arriving in the United States, I could never have guessed that the tour would be the beginning of the end of my time in King Crimson.

The first show we played in America was on 29 October 1969 at Goddard College in Plainfield, Vermont. Dee Anthony had chosen this particular venue because he wanted to protect us. It was so far out of the way that it was unlikely that the music critics from the major cities would bother to make the trip.

We flew up to Vermont courtesy of what Dee used to affectionately call 'Sudden Death Airlines'. It was an old two-propeller plane of the type that Buddy Holly and Otis Redding had crashed in. We all boarded the plane with trepidation. After being delayed on the runway for twenty nail-biting minutes we took off from La Guardia in New York, which was then followed by an hour of bouncing around in the ominous dark grey clouds before we finally arrived in snow-covered Vermont.

As we stepped outside the airport terminal, we were greeted by a couple of college students who helped to bundle our luggage into the back of two waiting estate cars. I was struck by a word that was written in sweeping chrome letters along the side of one of the cars. It was one of those peculiar moments when one single iconic image just says it all, and what it was saying to me was that here I was, in the United States of America, the home of Elvis Presley, John Wayne and Little Richard. From Florida to Hollywood and from hot dogs to hurricanes, the United States has it all and I still get that same feeling to this day, every time I enter the country. The word on the side of the car was 'Chevrolet'.

We set off for the show with the two young students in the front and the rest of us sitting in the rear, feeling grateful to be back on the ground. After a few miles, the road began to climb up a steep hill. We twisted and turned along snowy, tree-lined roads before we eventually came upon a charming little village that had a couple of convenience stores, a small garage and few wooden chalets dotted around. As we drove through the village, we happened to spot a community notice board with a large poster advertising a concert – 'King Curtis Appearing Live' – that was taking place at the local college where we were about to perform. We thought no more about it and drove on.

Daylight was starting to fade and we followed the road through a heavily wooded area and then down a gravel track, where we saw a few students walking around. We arrived at a brightly lit building, which turned out to be the college gymnasium, opposite the main school. We could see through the windows that a small stage had been erected at one end and that all of our gear had been set up, waiting for us.

After a brief sound check we were shown into a small changing room behind the stage where we waited for show time to arrive. From the dressing room, we could hear all the students entering the hall and shouting to each other as they began organising themselves places to sit. There was no proper seating in the gymnasium so everyone sat festival-style on the floor. When it was show time, the main gymnasium lights were turned off and our small stage lights, which were a few red household fire-glow bulbs scattered on the floor, were switched on.

As we walked up on to the stage there was nervous, tentative applause. It was different from the expectant and enthusiastic reactions we had come to expect back in England. We pressed on regardless and began to play the opening number, '21st Century Schizoid Man'. Before the song had finished we saw three or four students suddenly jump up and run out of the hall in a panic. We didn't know what to think because the rest of the audience seemed enthusiastic.

The rest of the show went down well until we started to play the last song, 'Mars, the Bringer of War'. This piece opens in a sombre way with the snare drum tapping out the incessant five-four rhythm, which gets louder and louder throughout the entire piece. Robert would then join in playing the same rhythm while staring at the audience with menace and disdain. The intensity of the piece would build until the final staccato movement when two strobe lights would begin flashing in perfect sync with the music as Ian McDonald entered with the huge orchestral main theme on the Mellotron.

As I looked down at the audience, I could see terror on the faces of some of the students and another group of them got up and ran out of the hall in a panic. After the show had finished, we were informed that the kids who had run out had taken LSD earlier in the evening, and what had made it even worse was that they were not expecting to see King Crimson at all. They had come to see King Curtis, a rhythm and blues act we had seen advertised on the poster back down in the village. No wonder some of them were freaked out, losing themselves in their trips and expecting to hear some laidback soul music, only to be assaulted by '21st Century Schizoid Man' and 'Mars, the Bringer of War'. It turned out that the college printer had made a mistake and had put the wrong name on the poster.

Our next destination was Boston and, much to the relief of Michael and Ian in particular, we were told that we could drive there rather than travel courtesy of Sudden Death Airlines. We were booked to perform three nights at the Boston Tea Party, an underground venue often used by artists such as the Velvet Underground, the Grateful Dead and Frank Zappa. We then moved on to Chicago, the home of Al Capone, prohibition and, of course, the blues. For us, it was right up there with New York and Los Angeles as one of the iconic cities of the United States. We had come to know and love it from television programmes such *The Untouchables* with Eliot Ness and from the blues and big band recordings we had heard over the years.

After we checked into the downtown Chicago Holiday Inn,

a lady from the front desk called my room and insisted I come back down to the lobby. I asked her what the problem was.

'Oh, my lord,' she replied. 'Just get down here right now.'

I jumped off the bed and put on a pair of sweatpants, and headed for the elevator. As I stepped out into the lobby I looked straight ahead and in one jaw-dropping moment everything became horribly clear. Our equipment truck had crashed into the front of the hotel.

It turned out that the road crew had rented a huge Avis truck to move the equipment around and when they drove up to the hotel they forgot that the truck was much taller than the regular car they were used to driving. The top of the truck crashed into the canopy roofing that covered the entrance to the foyer, and the vehicle got stuck so far under the roof that the crew were not able to reverse it back out. So, there it stood among the debris of bricks, broken glass, dust and rubble.

'It would appear we've had a slight issue with the roof,' said Vick Vickers, one of our road managers. 'But don't worry, everything is being taking care of.'

There was certainly nothing I could do, so I went back to my room and waited for the afternoon call to go down to the venue for a sound check. We were playing at the Kinetic Playground, a converted old theatre. When we arrived, Dee came up to us in the foyer and told us to hang back for a moment. He diverted us into a side room and we closed the door behind us. Outside we could hear shouting. I asked Dee what was happening and he explained that there was a dispute between the promoter and some people who had been demanding protection money. Dee thought that they might even be the police.

After a few minutes, it went quiet and Dee went outside to find out what was happening. When he returned, he told us there was nothing to worry about. The people offering the protection had threatened to burn the place to the ground if the promoter didn't pay up, but it seemed that the matter had been resolved. Dee then smiled and said: 'Welcome to Chicago!'

He took us up to the stage for the sound check and we listened to the headline act. It was Iron Butterfly and they were playing their famous song, 'In-A-Gadda-Da-Vida'.

When the show started, our support slot overran and we couldn't get our gear off the stage before Iron Butterfly were due on, so we had to leave it up there on stage. The road crew were told that they should load out early the following morning.

The next day began with another distressed phone call. This time it was from one of the road managers telling me to get down to the venue as quickly as possible. There had been a fire in the theatre overnight.

We assembled in the lobby and set off for the venue. I will always remember walking into the foyer of what remained of the Kinetic Playground and being struck by the acrid smell of burning rubber. We climbed over the fire hoses that were still in place in case the fire restarted. As we entered the theatre area, I saw all of our formerly beautiful new equipment still standing where we had left it, but the speakers had melted out of their charred cabinets and the Mellotron was reduced to a pile of ashes and a skeletal metal frame. It was clear to us all that the dispute of a day earlier hadn't been resolved, after all.

At that point, we were convinced the tour would be over. But this was the United States and things move fast. Within twenty-four hours our entire back line, including the Mellotron, had been replaced and the tour continued on to Motor City Detroit, where we performed on 12, 13 and 14 November 1969 at both the Grand Riviera and the legendary Eastown Theatre. After a few days off, we started the second leg of the tour at the Fillmore East, New York, on 21 and 22 November for the promoter Bill Graham. Bill was both loved and feared in equal measure, and went on to become perhaps the greatest rock promoter of all time. He was referred to by Dee and by our booking agent Frank Barsalona as 'The Mouth'.

I soon realised why Bill got that nickname when I started to talk to him – he was a larger-than-life character with a wide, cartoon mouth and he shouted all the time. He was a lovely man, though, and I have no doubt that the formula behind his astounding success was simply his honest love and enthusiasm for music. At heart, the great people who were involved in King Crimson's American tour had one essential thing in common: they were passionate about music – music as art first, business second. That is not to say that the business was unimportant, but they were led by the heart. They looked for the talent, they believed in the talent, then they sold the talent, and that's the way it worked.

Dee, Frank and Bill were close friends and between the three of them, plus our record company boss in the States, the legendary Ahmet Ertegün of Atlantic Records, you can trace a direct link from this group to almost every successful artist in the American music industry: Bob Dylan, the Beatles, the Who, U2, Bruce Springsteen, ELP, Joe Cocker, the Rolling Stones, Aretha Franklin, Ray Charles, Led Zeppelin . . . the list goes on.

In terms of live music, rock and roll was just about package tours and fifteen-minute sets before Frank Barsalona came along. 'At that time, rock was lower than the rodeo,' he would say. It was Frank who introduced a brand-new creed of honesty and ethics into the music business and transformed live music performance art into the modern, well-organised business that it is today.

When these men got together it was challenging – and hilarious – to be around them. The energy level was so intense. If you didn't know who they were, you would assume that they were having a screaming argument. It seemed that the whole point of the discussion was to see who could deliver the best insult. They would spend the first five minutes demeaning each other – Bill Graham would be calling Frank 'a flesh peddler' – and then they would say what they had to say. It's a New York thing – there are some restaurants where even the waiters insult you. But these meetings always ended up the same way, with laughter and hugging and kisses on the cheeks.

The Fillmore East shows were fantastic. We were supporting Joe Cocker and the audience were eager to see this new band from England who everyone was making such a fuss over. This was the moment we had been waiting for. Here we were – at last – performing in New York City, the Big Apple.

After we had finished playing I watched Joe perform. It was remarkable seeing how he writhed and contorted and hung on to the microphone stand in an effort to remain upright as he sung 'With a Little Help from My Friends'. Despite being the worse for wear, he sounded great and the audience loved him.

We headed down to Florida to play the Palm Beach Festival on a bill also featuring the Rolling Stones and Janis Joplin. This was the first open-air festival that the band had played in the United States and we didn't know what to expect. We had done a few festival shows in England at racecourses and public parks but this was on an entirely different scale.

The first shock happened during the take-off in a little bubble-glass helicopter which was being used to shuttle artists to the festival site about thirty miles away. I had never flown in a helicopter before so it was a heart-stopping moment when it rose vertically and began soaring over the buildings below. The pilot had just returned from a tour of duty in Vietnam and was taking real pleasure in demonstrating how he could throw his chopper around.

We touched down at the festival site and were bundled out of the helicopter. Dust and dry grass were blowing into our eyes as we were pulled away from beneath the rotating blades, but I could see that someone lying on a stretcher was immediately being loaded on to the helicopter. As soon as we were at a safe distance, I asked one of the stretcher bearers what had happened. Over the noise of the rotor, I heard him shout: 'Rattlesnake! Bitten by a rattlesnake under the stage!'

We were relieved to get back to the hotel safely that night.

At breakfast the following morning, Janis Joplin was sitting alone at a table. She had a half-empty bottle of Jack Daniels in her lap. She looked up as I entered the room and we nodded and smiled to each other but her head fell back down and we sat in silence. I felt dreadfully sorry for her but there was nothing I could do. I went back up to my room to pack my bags and get ready to leave for the next stop on our tour: Los Angeles, the city of the fallen angels.

There is a special feeling I get when arriving at LAX. No matter how many times I visit Los Angeles, I always take a moment outside the airport to stop and savour the waving palms, the warm breeze and the clear blue sky. On that first visit, the next thing that struck me, while we were driving into LA, was the sight of all the working oil wells with rock-ing-horse pumps that keep pumping the oil day and night. I had never seen anything like it. It emphasised to me that LA may sometimes seem to be a shallow place full of people seeking stardom, but it was built by pioneers whose spirit lives on in the hearts of some of the old Californian residents to this day.

When we arrived at our hotel, the Sunset Marquis, the road manager and I went straight up to my room to take a look at it as we would be staying there for a whole week. As we opened the door, I saw that there was a large ice bucket containing what appeared to be two bottles of wine on the dining table. *What better time to celebrate than right now?* I thought.

The road manager opened one of the bottles and filled a couple of glasses. We drank the first glass straight down and he poured us both another. After they were finished, we had another half a glass each and then I realised that I needed to go to the bathroom. I can remember pushing open the door but the rest is a blank until I woke up on the bed with a huge black eye and a searing hangover.

I discovered the 'wine' had actually been mescal – the spirit similar to tequila – and after opening the bathroom door I had blacked out and hit my head on the side of the bath. The worst thing about having the black eye was not the pain or temporary loss of vision. It was about having to go through the same laborious explanation every time I met someone new. 'Oh dear, how did you get that?' they would say. Or 'I bet that hurt!' I had to endure this for a week as we played our five-night run on 3–7 December at the Whiskey a Go Go on Sunset Boulevard.

These were not the best shows we did in the States. Although the band played well, the show times were later than usual and by the time we came on stage most of the audience were out of it and in bad shape. The finer moments of the band's performance were lost on them. Although this was the wrong venue for an act like King Crimson to perform in, we did manage to kick-start our reputation on the West Coast. Those people who could actually remember being there enjoyed the show and helped to spread the word.

My time in the band, however, was coming to an end.

The last performances by the original King Crimson line-up took place at Bill Graham's Fillmore West in San Francisco in mid-December 1969. On the same bill were the Nice and the Chambers Brothers.

When we arrived, Ian McDonald and Michael Giles made the sudden announcement that they had decided to leave the band and stop touring. There were never any musical differences between the members of the band: they just wanted to concentrate on a studio career instead. I knew that neither of them liked flying – and we had endured a few unnerving flights by then – but I had not realised that the rest of the travelling and the general mayhem and intensity of touring had become such a decisive issue for them. They wanted to retreat from the circus of being in a rapidly successful touring band.

Soon after we had heard the news, Robert came to my room. I said to Robert, 'If you want to form a new band, we can do that. I'll be happy to form a new band.' But he told me that he would like to continue on with the name King Crimson and wanted to find replacements for Ian and Michael. I didn't agree with him. King Crimson was all about the magical chemistry between the original people involved and the idea of bringing in two new people and pretending that nothing had happened just didn't feel right to me. Ian had made a massive contribution to the band both as a writer and a performer while Michael's drumming was so unusual it was essential to the King Crimson sound.

I left the meeting with Robert feeling depressed. A bright light had shone for a brief period of time, but now it was all over. The King was dead.

After our last show at Fillmore West had finished, on 15 December, I returned to the hotel and just as I was walking through the lobby I ran into Tony Stratton-Smith, the manager of the Nice. We had a few brief words and he told me that Keith Emerson was in the bar and that he would like to meet with me. I had been struck by Keith Emerson's playing and stage presence when I had stayed to watch the Nice's sound check. So I told Tony that, yes, I would go down and see Keith after I had made a couple of phone calls back to England.

When I arrived at the bar, Keith and I shook hands warmly and I sat down beside him and we began to chat. There was an immediate sense of compatibility, as we both drew upon European music for the roots of our inspiration rather than the blues or Motown or gospel. He asked me how things were going with King Crimson and I told him that, despite our incredible early success, the band was about to split up. He said that he was also thinking about moving on, having become creatively exhausted in the Nice.

'We should consider forming a band together,' he said.

Part Two

CHAPTER 5

Emerson, Lake & Palmer

I arrived back in London on 16 December 1969. The tour of the United States had been bittersweet. On the one hand, I had enjoyed all the new experiences and met fascinating people: the United States had taken me to its heart and in turn I had started to fall in love with it. On the other, the great young band that I had formed with my friend Robert Fripp had come to a sad and premature end. And in a final twist, a new door had just opened up, with the exciting prospect of working with Keith Emerson. It was a strange and rather bewildering experience.

I knew about Keith before playing on the same bill as him at the Fillmore West. The Nice, like King Crimson, had been causing a bit of a sensation. I don't think that many people remember that they were originally the backing group for the soul singer P. P. Arnold. Things really took off for them when

Keith started experimenting on keyboards and reworked Leonard Bernstein's 'America' from *West Side Story*. There was a lot of fuss when he burned the American flag on the stage of the Royal Albert Hall – some American radio stations refused to play 'America'.

By the time King Crimson and the Nice were playing on the same bill in the States, the Nice's set list would include reworkings of some Bob Dylan songs together with versions of Bach and Tchaikovsky pieces. Meanwhile, King Crimson were mixing together Holst's *The Planets*, quite heavy rock, jazz and folk, and the two bands together were spearheading what would become the progressive rock scene. But, like King Crimson, there was some unhappiness in the band. In their case, there were musical differences and changes in the line-up, and Keith was beginning to feel that no one else in the band could spur him on creatively.

Keith was thinking of scrapping the Nice and starting again before we got to know each other. He had already asked Tony Stratton-Smith who was the best bass player in the United Kingdom, and Tony had brought up my name. While we were on the same bill in the States, Keith, it turned out, had been keeping an eye on me, thinking about the future. Apparently, he wasn't sure what to make of me, disagreeing with some of my opinions – he always would – but he could tell that we shared something in our approach to music.

Very shortly after I arrived back home, Keith came round to visit me in my basement flat near Sloane Square in London.

We chatted for a while and I played him some music that I was particularly fond of from my record collection. I think this was the first time Keith heard Aaron Copland's *Fanfare for the Common Man*. We sat there for some hours and played through various pieces of music all the way from Bach to Dave Grusin, a composer and pianist of whom I am still very fond to this day. Keith was quite surprised by the diversity of music I had in my collection and it also formed a really good basis for our discussions regarding a future musical direction with which we would both feel comfortable.

During our initial discussions, we decided to try and keep the band down to a three-piece and in order to achieve that we would need to find the perfect drummer. The first person I thought of was the great Mitch Mitchell, who had recently become available due to the break-up of the Jimi Hendrix Experience.

I called Mitch on the phone and a couple of days later he came around to see me. He arrived with his personal road manager and, after we said our initial hellos, I offered them both a drink and we sat down facing each other across a coffee table. I started talking to Mitch and telling him how much I had always enjoyed his work with Jimi, when all of a sudden out of the corner of my eye I noticed that a handgun had been placed on the table.

For a moment, my eyes flashed back and forth between Mitch, the gun and the road manager, and Mitch could obviously see that I was uncomfortable. He laughed a little awkwardly and told me not to worry – the road manager just carried the weapon for their personal protection. I asked the road manager if he wouldn't mind just putting it away while we were talking, and he kindly obliged.

We stayed chatting for a while and had almost finished when Mitch turned back towards me and said, 'You know, maybe we should all get together with Jimi and have a jam. You never know how things might work out.'

'Sounds good,' I said as we got up to shake hands.

After Mitch left, I reflected on what he had said and decided that, as much as I loved Jimi, the idea of having too many strong players trying to do something radical in one band would probably be a bridge too far.

The following day, I phoned Keith and told him about the meeting I'd had with Mitch and about the strange incident of the gun being placed on the table. I remember Keith being quite surprised because we both knew Mitch to be a really laid-back and peaceful guy. I think it was just a little bit of silly bravado, but it was disconcerting. During the latter part of Jimi's life, through no fault of his own, he had got mixed up with some less than savoury characters in the States and per-haps a bit of their gangster posturing had rubbed off on Mitch and the road manager. We decided that we had better con-tinue our search for a drummer just in case things didn't work out with Mitch. As it turned out, Mitch didn't join the band and we never did jam with Jimi – Jimi died soon afterwards, in September 1970.

A couple of days after I met Mitch, we got a call from Robert Stigwood, the manager of Cream and the Bee Gees, who had heard we were forming a band. He told us that there was an outstanding drummer by the name of Carl Palmer that he had come across, and he thought he would be a perfect match.

He explained that, although Carl was only twenty, he had already played with Chris Farlowe and the Thunderbirds, the Crazy World of Arthur Brown and his own band Atomic Rooster, and Robert felt that he was eager to develop musically and was capable of much more. Atomic Rooster had released a debut album in February 1970 and were pretty successful – there had been a change of singer but Carl says he was relatively happy at the time Keith phoned him in May of that year.

A few days later, we arranged to meet up with Carl in a small rehearsal studio in Soho Square in London's West End. As soon as Carl walked into the room it was clear that he was an extremely bright young guy with a very effervescent personality. It was also very easy to see by the way he went about setting up his drum kit that he had the mindset of a professional player.

From the very first few bars we played together, I could sense there was a very special chemistry between the three of us. We started with 'Rondo', which Keith had adapted from Dave Brubeck's jazz classic, 'Blue Rondo à la Turk', for the Nice's first album. While we were playing, I looked across at

Keith – it was clear that he had also immediately realised that this was the drummer we had been looking for.

For a few days after that, Carl played hard to get even though he knew that this was one of those offers that only comes along once in a lifetime. Carl still likes to tell the story of how I called him in the end and told him that if he didn't join the band he would not only be hurting himself but would be hurting me as well. My determination may have helped to push him along, but he does say that he finally worked out that perhaps the musicians in Atomic Rooster were not good enough to take him to where he wanted to be. The next day he joined and the band was complete.

The first thing we needed was a name for the new band so we all put on our thinking caps and started to look for something appropriate.

We initially came up with a few different names but none of them sounded right. If a band name does not really suit the music, it can sound dreadful. It's rather like calling a dog Graham. After a great deal of soul searching, we eventually came to the conclusion that the reason we were having such trouble was that we had all come from such well-known bands that somehow these past identities were not sitting easily with anything new.

It was then that I think Keith suggested just using our own names. After just a few moments of consideration, we all agreed that 'Emerson, Lake & Palmer' sounded right and so that would be the name of the band. Perhaps it sounded a bit like a firm of accountants or lawyers, but it turned out all right.

It is interesting now just to reflect back on exactly how ELP came into being. Unlike the Beatles or the Stones, we were not old school pals or local kids who happened to meet up on the train or bus on their way home. ELP had really been created by the destiny of our earlier bands and although we didn't realise it at the time, this would have some quite profound implications a little further down the line when the word 'supergroup' was being applied to us due to our previous successes.

We never had the chance to develop the band organically before we were being labelled. ELP were often portrayed as if we had all been born with silver spoons in our mouths, which of course was a very long way from the truth. All three members of ELP had spent many hard years in former bands sleeping in the back of vans and quite literally living on the breadline. We had paid our dues in the early days in order to get to where we were, so this tag of being a supergroup was not something we either wanted or felt good about.

It was this tag, added to the fact that a lot of the music we played had European classical roots, that probably gave some people the impression that we were being pretentious or high-minded. It was certainly true that we were ambitious and we did want to be original and innovative. However, at no time did we ever claim to be classical musicians or even classically trained musicians – we were just British rock-and-roll musicians drawing a large part of our influence from European rather than American roots. For us, it seemed important at the time to try and break away from the same old tried and tested path that so many other British rock acts had followed in the past by using American blues, rock and roll and gospel music as their sole source of inspiration.

By taking this approach, we left our mark on the history of rock music, but I will always have a certain amount of regret somewhere deep down inside, particularly as a singer, at not having been able to embrace American soul, blues and country music in my career as much as I would have liked.

When ELP was formed, such was the buzz around the band that expectations were very quickly flying high and within days we were being asked for a date when we thought we could deliver the first album. None of us really had any material written at that time and it was fast becoming obvious that there wasn't really going to be a whole lot of time to prepare any. Because of the good experience I had enjoyed with Chris Blackwell, we were happy to sign to Island Records and immediately started preparing to record our first album.

Due to the fact that we had such a short time to prepare the material, it was mostly made up of things that Keith and I still had locked away in the vaults from the past. This is one of the reasons that the album did not really have a descriptive title. The album when it came out was simply entitled *Emerson, Lake & Palmer*, which we thought was the most honest way to step out and move forward.

While all this was going on in 1970, Pete Sinfield increased his involvement in King Crimson because Robert Fripp was the only member. I believe that there was some talk about asking Elton John to be the singer, but he had just recorded his second solo album, which included 'Your Song' and was about to become a big hit. Although I was no longer in the band, I ended up singing on every vocal track but one of their second album, *In the Wake of Poseidon*, which was recorded from January to April 1970 at Wessex Sound Studios and released in May of that year.

The album begins with an acapella 'Peace – A Beginning' and concludes with 'Peace – An End', and features the eight-minute title track and 'Pictures of a City', a version of 'A Man, a City', which King Crimson used to play on tour in 1969 before Michael, Ian and myself all left the band. The only song in which I didn't feature on *In the Wake of Poseidon* was 'Cadence and Cascade', which Robert's old friend from Dorset, Gordon Haskell, recorded, and there were a couple of instrumental tracks, 'Peace – A Theme' and 'The Devil's Triangle', as well.

The Giles brothers worked as session musicians on the album, and the three of us ended up performing the single 'Cat Food' with Robert and the jazz pianist Keith Tippett on *Top of the Pops*. *In the Wake of Poseidon* proved to be King Crimson's highest-charting album in the UK, which is a bit bizarre as most of the people who performed on it were not even in the band at the time it was made.

As it turned out, this would not be the last King Crimson album that I would appear on. A four-CD live album called *Epigraph* was released in 1997 and features the 1969 perform-ances at Fillmore East and Fillmore West in the United States and at the Ninth National Jazz and Blues Festival and the Chesterfield Jazz Club in the United Kingdom, as well as a live session we did for BBC Radio. The recordings include some of our best music together, including '21st Century Schizoid Man', 'The Court of the Crimson King' and 'Mars', as well as 'A Man, a City'.

It's funny to think that during most of the performances captured on that album, I was playing away enthusiastically with a band that had great material and seemed to be going places fast, but I had no idea it was all about to end. As the album also includes songs from that very final concert at Fillmore West, I sometimes wonder whether you can tell that I knew it was all over just from the sound of my voice and the way I played the bass.

The early recording sessions for *Emerson, Lake & Palmer* took place at the Island recording studios in Basing Street near Portobello Road. We quickly changed studios to Advision in Gosfield Street, Fitzrovia, and it turned out to be a fortuitous move for us. It was equipped with state-of-the-art equipment but, more importantly, this was where we first met Eddy Offord. He was a first-class recording engineer and incredibly dedicated, too. Most nights, after everyone had gone home, Eddy and I would sit down at the recording desk and work on the rough mixes until daybreak. I was the producer of the album, with input from both Keith and Carl, but having Eddy there was fantastic. Keith would always say that the band never really made a decision that I would be the producer – I think I just naturally sat at the desk because I already had some experience with King Crimson – but he did acknowledge that it turned out well.

The band had a sense that the music we were making on this album was meaningful, and that it might even be successful as well. Our style of music is, of course, known as 'progressive' but this was not a term we used at the time. Like King Crimson, we just saw ourselves as an innovative band who were going to break free from the conventions of the industry. The experimentation we had done in our previous bands would be taken to a new level. We certainly were not going be a singles band.

One of my songs on the album did turn out to be a hit single, though, and it all happened by accident. At first, I had no plans to bring 'Lucky Man' to the group. We already had a fairly simple song on the album, 'Take a Pebble', which I wrote very early on with Keith before Carl had joined the band, and we built it up with a piano solo for Keith and a guitar solo for me. The other tracks on the album were more complicated, though, including 'The Barbarian' inspired by Béla Bartók's 'Allegro Barbaro', and 'Knife-Edge', which merged elements of Janáček's *Sinfonietta* and Bach's 'French Suite in D Minor' – those pieces showed how we were trying to draw on European classical influences to create a radical new sound. 'The Three Fates' and 'Tank' showed off the musical virtuosity of Keith and Carl respectively, with 'The Three Fates' involving us lugging all the recording equipment to both the Royal Festival Hall and a church in Finchley to capture Keith's organ solos.

'Lucky Man', however, didn't seem to break new ground and was very simple in its approach. This isn't how Keith remembers it, but that day remains very clear in my mind. As the recording sessions were about to draw to a close, we counted how much of the album's running time we had left. We discovered to our dismay that we were over three minutes short. (During the glorious days of vinyl, the prescribed time for a record was twenty-one minutes per side.)

Eddy's voice came over the talkback.

'We need one last song,' he said.

Carl asked if anyone had any ideas. We looked at each other blankly and there was a pregnant silence until I reluctantly came forward.

'Well, if there's nothing else, I do have this little folk song that I wrote when I was a kid,' I said.

The awkwardness in the studio returned until Keith said: 'Okay, why don't you play it and let's take a listen?'

I put down my bass, picked up my Gibson J200 and sang the song. For a couple of minutes, Keith tried to improvise along on the Hammond organ but he ran out of ideas. He suggested that I just record it on my own. I was a bit surprised. It was such a straightforward song, after all, so it allowed plenty of room for him to come up with something. What was the problem? I could see he wasn't keen, though, so I agreed to carry on without him. Keith left to go to the pub down the road from the studio.

I took my J200 into the isolated vocal booth and got ready to record the song. Suddenly the padded door opened and Carl poked his head around.

'Do you want me to play along on drums?' he asked.

I gave him the thumbs up and a few minutes later we had recorded the first take. We went back into the control room to take a listen. It didn't sound great. We started analysing what was wrong but Eddy suggested that I record the bass track before we got overly critical. So I did, and then I added the backing vocals and the electric guitar solo as well.

I was never tempted to revise the lyrics. Over time, people would interpret the song in various ways. Some people associated it with the last years of the Vietnam War and a soldier getting shot, others with the assassination of John F. Kennedy. It seemed to evoke the tumultuous era we had been living through. But that was never my intention. The lyrics were simply a medieval fantasy I had written as a child.

When Keith returned from the pub and we played him the track, he was shocked to hear how this modest folk song had been transformed into such a rich and powerful track.

'Well,' he said, 'perhaps it would be good if I played on it, after all.'

We all laughed. I was happy that he was enthusiastic about playing on the song but the problem now was I had just covered the solo part of the song on electric guitar. The only space left for him was the long fade-out at the end of the song. We started to think about what sound would be best to use.

'How about trying out the Moog synthesiser?' said Keith.

We had seen this new piece of equipment being delivered earlier in the day. Bob Moog had sent it and it looked more like a telephone switchboard than a musical instrument.

'What does it sound like?' I asked.

'I don't really know. I've never used it in a studio.'

So we agreed to give it a go anyway.

Keith went back into the studio and started to experiment with the sounds.

Eddy and I sat in the control room listening as Keith slowly brought this machine to life. We started to hear this fascinating swooping sound, a portamento whereby the pitch slides from one note to another, and we suggested to Keith that we should run the track alongside it. When experimenting in a recording studio, it is always worth capturing the first performance just case something extraordinary happens. So many magic moments have been lost in studios over the years because that first pass wasn't recorded. Fortunately, this was not the case here and, as the run-through started, we punched

84

the track into record. As the track came to an end, I turned to Eddy and said: 'Is it just me or did that sound really good?'

Eddy smiled. 'Let's listen back,' he said.

Over the studio talkback I told Keith to come in and take a listen. He insisted that he was only just getting started and that he was sure he could do a better take. However, the track we had used to record him on was the last one available. To do a second take would mean scrubbing the one he had just recorded. I couldn't bring myself to do it. Keith would later say he was devastated about this but we managed to talk him round and he agreed to take a listen.

As soon as he heard it in context, there was no question about it. We all knew then that it was special. Keith would say that I was always better than him at choosing which of his solo takes to use – he was too close to the music and always thought he could do a better take, but later he would agree that it was impossible to imagine a better solo for a particular track than the one I had chosen.

Of course, the Moog has now become one of the most famous synthesisers of all time, but this was the pop break-through for the instrument. As Kurt Loder of MTV would later say: '"Lucky Man" demonstrated for delighted keyboard players everywhere that it was at last possible for them to blow amp-shredding lead guitarists right off the stage, if they so chose.'

So that was it. 'Lucky Man' was finished and ELP's first album was complete.

CHAPTER 6

What a Circus

The spirit of the band at that time was extremely strong and in some ways it felt like a coiled spring just waiting to be released. Although we had really enjoyed recording the first album it was nevertheless clear to us at the time that the real moment of truth as far as audience reaction was concerned was going to be based on the band's ability to perform live.

As the recording sessions for the first album came to a close, our managers E. G. Management booked our first UK tour. Luckily, they were able to get us a slot to perform at the now legendary Isle of Wight Festival in 1970, and we knew it would be a real platform for us to show the world what we were capable of. We were extremely excited to have this incredible opportunity so early on in the band's career, but at the same time we were quite nervous about playing at such a big event before we even had a chance to get the show broken in and under control. In this sense, it really was a trial by fire.

Having had a good deal of experience in playing live shows with our previous bands, we had the good sense to insist on having our inaugural show somewhere a bit more out of the way and less conspicuous, so the very first show of ELP took place in front of 800 people at the Guildhall in Plymouth on Sunday 23 August 1970.

We were nervous. I had barely performed in front of an audience since December 1969 and Carl and Keith had both been away from the stage for a few months, too. And here we were, playing live together for the very first time as well as playing material no one had ever heard before: 'The Barbarian', 'Take a Pebble' and the full-length, three-quarters-of-an-hour version of 'Pictures at an Exhibition', as well as 'Rondo'. Keith kicked off the concert with the simple words: 'This is what we sound like.'

We ended up getting a fifteen-minute standing ovation and I felt a deep sense of relief as I drove back home to London.

There is a saying that 'a day is a long time in politics' and sometimes the same can also be said of music. For ELP, the 'longest day' would almost certainly be Saturday 29 August 1970. On that day, we performed our second show to an audience of over 600,000 people at the Isle of Wight Festival.

The roster of artists appearing there was truly awe-inspiring: Jimi Hendrix, the Who, Miles Davis, Leonard Cohen, Sly and

ith my mother, Pearl.

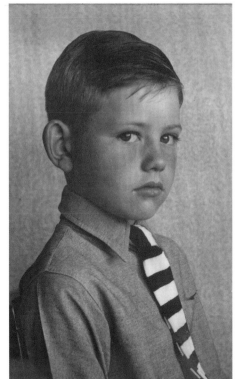

Me aged six.

(left) My grandfather Bruno Parsons who rode in the Grand National and, on one occasion, was asked by Winston Churchill to referee his polo match!

(above) Me aged eleven.

OAKDALE SCHOOL

REPORT ....AUTUMN........ Term, 19 56.

NAME ..GREGORY..LAKE....................................... CLASS ..8a..

	Exam Mark	Exam Max.	Term Mark	Term Max.	Position	Remarks
ARITHMETIC	55	80	62	100	25	Far more care and concentration needed. Dawdles and falls behind class.
MENTAL	13	20				
ENGLISH	34	60	75	100	12.	Careless and often very untidy. Wastes time and is always one of the last to finish.
READING	19	20				
SPELLING	15	20				
HISTORY	18	25				Should be better Must concentrate fully
GEOGRAPHY	18.	25				
ART	Fair		MUSIC	Average		
HANDWORK	Fair RJK		NEEDLEWORK			
GAMES	Fair					
TOTALS	172	250	137	200.	Final Total	309/450.

CONDUCT: Often very irritating but can be very good and helpful.

GENERAL REMARKS: Gregory needs constant urging to make him work. Carelessness in thinking and writing has spoilt most of his work this term.

POSITION IN CLASS....18....out of....41 (8 not classified having missed some tests)

POSITION IN AGE GROUP IN ARITHMETIC & ENGLISH....46th....out of....142.

E. Beresford .... Class Teacher

W. Maccall Boyd. .... Head Master

Next Term commences....9th January, 1957.

My school report from 1956, where I was given an 'average' in Music. I was later told by the careers master that playing the guitar was not a job and that I would end up on the scrap heap.

Don Strike's shop. Don was my guitar teacher for two and a half years and a major influence on my career. He also taught my friend Robert Fripp.

hen I was in Unit 4, we used to travel around in a converted ambulance which was useful for
ffic jams as it still had the emergency bell.

ith my Shame bandmates. *(left to right)* Me, Jon Petterssen, Billy Nims and Malcolm Brasher.

Me with Hank B. Marvin. From the moment I first hea[rd] 'Apache', Hank was one of m[y] greatest inspirations and it wa[s] Hank who ignited my vision of becoming a professional musician.

Me with Robert Fripp, who asked me to be lead singer and bass guitarist in his new band, King Crimson.

LP with Miles Davis. *(© Neil Preston)*

With my roadie Brian Magoo and dogs Fluffy *(left)*, Cromwell *(right)* and Rufus *(front)* at home in Windelsham. *(© Kenny Smith)*

Walking back to the dressing room with Carl after one of our Madison Square Garden concerts in December 1973. *(© Neil Preston)*

With Keith in the back of our limousine. *(© Neil Preston)*

(left) With Regina on our wedding day, 5th January 1974.

(above) On honeymoon in Ojai, California.
(© Neil Preston)

(left) With Regina and Natasha. You can see Ahmet Ertegun, head of Atlantic Records, in the background.
(© Kenny Smith)

Lucky Man

He had white horses and ladies by the score
All dressed in satin and waiting by the door

Oh what a lucky man he was
Oh what a lucky man he was

White lace and feathers they made up his bed
A gold covered mattress on which he was laid

Oh what a lucky man he was
Oh what a lucky man he was

He went to fight wars for his country and his king
Of his honour and his glory the people would sing

Oh what a lucky man he was
Oh what a lucky man he was

A bullet had found him his blood ran as he cried
No money could save him so he laid down and he died

Oh what a lucky man he was
Oh what a lucky man he was

Greg Lake.
333/750

'Lucky Man'.

the Family Stone, Joni Mitchell, the Doors, Jethro Tull, the Moody Blues and many more. And here we were, this almost completely unknown band, Emerson, Lake & Palmer. It could not have been a better launch pad.

We sensed an atmosphere of barely controlled chaos from the moment we arrived. Like most of these early epic rock festivals, the backstage area was complete pandemonium: people running around and panicking; medical emergencies taking place against the constant din of stage managers pleading and howling abuse over their walkie-talkies as the band on stage typically ran over their allotted time slot. Just as we arrived, we heard that the police were threatening to shut down the entire event.

Eventually the time came for us to perform and we were called to the steps at the side of the stage. As the MC started his announcement, we walked up the steps and out on to the stage itself. The scene was almost biblical, or perhaps like some huge set-piece in a Cecil B. DeMille epic film. The audience stretched back almost as far as the eye could see.

As I looked out at the crowd, I was suddenly overcome by a very strange sense of detachment. I think it must have simply been the sight of the huge gathering I was facing while I was standing there with just a guitar in my hands. Somehow, I was going to have to step forward and entertain them. Then we started to play.

Of course, there had been no chance of undertaking any sound checks before the show, so it really was a question of just flying by the seat of our pants and hoping for the best.

During the first number, all kinds of things were going through my head simultaneously. How is the sound? Are the monitors working correctly? (They weren't.) Is the audience responding to the music? (They were.) All of this, of course, at the same time as actually performing the music, which I believe at that moment was 'The Barbarian', the first track from the album. Keith and I could not hear each other and Carl was trying to tie everything together based on the few snatches he could hear.

The rest of the performance passed by in a blur until the very end of our experimental arrangement of 'Pictures at an Exhibition', when Keith and I triggered the two cannons on stage. It was an unbelievable, once-in-a-lifetime moment when the entire audience rose to their feet and gave the band a standing ovation.

The very next day, ELP were being blasted across the front page of almost every daily newspaper and music magazine in the world, and most of the reviews were excellent. We were thrilled by this reaction, but I still remember one small thing that slightly bothered me at the time. One of the newspaper headlines used the word 'supergroup' for the very first time. The word 'supermodel' was already in circulation at the time, so some journalist must have thought it had a catchy ring about it. I think they meant well but I was immediately concerned that it made us appear rather removed from the real world of rock and roll. I was right to be wary as, later in the life of the band, some journalists used the supergroup tag to try and attack us for being somehow elite or pretentious.

The band continued on our first tour and, on the back of that Isle of Wight performance, the shows sold out and we received standing ovations every night. The tour continued in Europe during the following months and the legend of ELP as a formidable live band had begun. The *Emerson, Lake & Palmer* album came out in November 1970, received an excellent review in *Melody Maker* and reached number four in the charts. We knew by then that we were always going to have some detractors in the music press, no matter what we did, but we also knew we had a future as both a live and a studio band.

At that time, things began to move very fast indeed and it felt like new shows were being booked literally minute by minute. We played a number of shows in Germany, Austria and Switzerland, and the tour of Germany in particular threw new experiences our way, including when we flew to Bremen airport on 31 December 1970 to play the famous German TV show, *Beat-Club*. Our aeroplane was an old Lufthansa propeller plane, and when we landed we taxied up to the front of this old concrete building with a corrugated tin roof that was clearly also a relic from the Second World War. It all looked exactly the same as those black-and-white wartime images of Adolf Hitler disembarking from his own aeroplane. It was as if nothing had changed.

There, waiting to greet us, was the legendary German

promoter, the late Horst Lippmann of Lippmann and Rau, who had brought the blues legends Willie Dixon, Muddy Waters and Howlin' Wolf over to Europe, including the UK, in the 1960s, where they had a huge effect on the likes of Mick Jagger and Eric Clapton.

Horst was standing there by a car and, after a few warm handshakes, we jumped into his vehicle and began to drive out of the airfield. The first thing we all immediately noticed was how smooth and comfortable the car felt so we asked him what make it was. A one-word answer came back: 'Mercedes,' said Horst with a huge smile on his face.

After we left the airport, we drove on to the autobahn – the forerunner of what we now refer to as the freeway or motorway. Very soon the car was moving along at over 90 mph – the autobahn had no speed limits.

Our expectation was that, because Germany had lost the war, things would have been poorer, or perhaps less good than they were back home. Once we had left the airport, it came as quite a shock for us to see just how advanced the Germans were, not only in terms of car manufacturing and road infra-structure, but also in the general quality of daily life, food, hotels and so on.

One of the German shows that will always stick in my mind was on the night of 29 November 1970 when we played in Munich at a venue called the Circus Krone. Despite the name, we had no real idea what this venue was. Sometimes you come across venues that take their name from some historical association like the corn exchange, assembly room or so on, and we just assumed that this would be the case in Munich – maybe it was named after some old Roman amphitheatre. However, when we arrived we were quite shocked to see that this was indeed an actual live working circus, complete with lions, tigers and elephants, and a sawdust-covered ring in the middle. Apparently, from time to time they would allow the venue to be used for music concerts and now ELP were about to perform there.

A stage had been built within the circus ring itself, and the audience was all around the stage, just as they would be when the real circus performed there.

The problems began when it became clear that someone had oversold the tickets. Halfway through the performance, a riot broke out in the crowd.

I went up to the microphone and tried to calm things down but unfortunately, due to the language barrier, the message just didn't get through. In fact, it just seemed to make things worse.

Eventually the sides of the tent opposite to the stage were opened up, revealing two fire trucks that immediately opened up with three or four powerful water cannons. As the jets of water blasted into the arena, people were being knocked off their feet and spun in all directions across the floor.

We had no choice other than to get off the stage as fast as we could and jump into the waiting cars backstage to make a speedy exit.

We had only performed half of the show but the water cannons, rather than our own cannons in 'Pictures at an Exhibition', had terminated the evening for good.

For weeks afterwards, no matter where we performed, our nostrils were filled with this awful smell of elephant as soon as we walked up on stage. In the end, we had to have all of the equipment deep cleaned in order to get rid of it.

After our first tour, the band's momentum was building at an incredible pace. It was obvious to all of us that we needed to record and deliver a new album as quickly as possible. We were already back in Advision Studios by January 1971, starting to record new music.

The debut album had been very successful, but it had not fully created a definitive style or template for us. It was largely made up of individual tracks and lacked an overall sense of cohesion. So, I suggested to Keith that we should develop an overarching concept for the second album.

We met at his house to exchange ideas. The two of us sat around the piano and the first thing he played me was this idea he had for a piano riff in five-four time. It was a repetitive, left-hand figure that continued to go round and round upon itself while the right hand performed an independent top-line melody.

My immediate impression was that it was a clever display of musical dexterity but it didn't provide a meaningful basis for a concept album. It sounded like a musical juggling act. From a lyricist's perspective, it didn't have the type of melody I could use as a starting point.

Since the advent of progressive music, there had been a tendency among certain musicians to try and impress the public by performing songs in odd time signatures. These pieces usually sounded gratuitous and self-indulgent to me, and I always thought that they were not as clever as they pretended to be. Often a piece claiming to be written in five-four time was just four-four with an added beat pasted at the end of each bar. A proper example of five-four, by contrast, would be 'Take Five' by Dave Brubeck or 'Mars, the Bringer of War' by Holst. Those pieces were conceived using five beats to the bar from the start.

So when Keith played the piano riff to me, I was wary that it might just sound like musical showboating. We could risk losing our musical integrity. I always believed in Keith's creative ability as a writer, but I was determined to try and protect the work we did together from becoming cheapened by pretention.

Keith felt strongly about keeping this riff, though, so I decided it would be better just to let it go and focus on other aspects of the album and its sound.

In the end, a complete musical concept was never developed for what became *Tarkus* so, personally, I wouldn't call it a concept album, although the songs are united by themes of science fiction, violence and the futility of war. Each separate piece is connected either by a musical transition or a seamless edit. The title and the cover images were simply retro-fitted after the recording had been completed.

The artist William Neal was given an acetate of *Tarkus* to listen to, and he developed the idea of the armadillo, other creatures and tank tracks along with Keith and myself. As for the title, Keith later said, according to Malcolm Dome's *Classic Rock Presents Prog*, that he wanted some kind of science-fiction name that 'represented Charles Darwin's theory of evolution in reverse. Some mutilation of the species caused by radiation . . . Tarkus!', but we only came up with that name after we had composed the music, so neither the title nor the artwork were part of the original concept. Of course, in the world of art anything can be viewed as a concept or a concept album. A red square painted on a white canvas entitled *Mud in Spring* is a concept if you choose to accept it as such and so it is with music. But in the case of *Tarkus*, it's skewing the facts a little bit. A concept album also might suggest that we were drawing on one source, one type of music, but when you listen to *Tarkus* you can hear that we weren't just tapping a single reservoir: classical, country, jazz, honky tonk and good old-fashioned rock and roll all played a part in creating the sound.

Despite my early concerns, I was very pleased with how *Tarkus* turned out. The playing, the production and the songs share a surreal quality that brought all the strands together. The twenty-minute 'Tarkus', made up of seven sections, takes up the whole first side, beginning with 'Eruption' and closing with 'Aquatarkus'. In between, there are short sections, written by Keith or the two of us together, plus 'Battlefield', which I wrote by myself. On 'Tarkus', Keith showed that he was taking the Moog to another level of inventiveness and Carl showed his drumming prowess – I'm not sure that there was another drummer in the world who could have done justice to it.

'Tarkus' became something of an ELP classic, and some of the six shorter pieces on the second side also became favourites – the jokey 'Jeremy Bender', with its country-style piano, was a regular of our live performances, and I like 'Bitches Crystal'. Keith and I co-wrote all but one of the tracks on the second side, and Carl co-wrote three of the tracks, including the rock-and-roll closer, 'Are You Ready Eddy?', our little tribute to the engineer Eddy Offord.

Some of the tracks relate to the direction we had started to take with 'The Barbarian' and 'Knife-Edge' on the first album, but on *Tarkus* the whole dark atmosphere and sound, as well as the musicianship, were more developed. On the first album, you could say that we were three individuals working together but obviously with different histories in different groups. Now, we started to sound like a band. We sounded like us.

Amazingly, in the light of how it takes some artists months or even years to record an album, we recorded the whole album in about two weeks – I think that reflects how well we were working as a band by that point. Everything was just flowing. I was the producer once more, and I felt that we were capturing something of the creative spirit of the band by working fast.

Tarkus was released on Island Records in the UK on 14 June 1971 and it became the first number one record I had ever made.

By then, we had already embarked upon our second European tour, which opened in Southampton on 4 March 1971.

Having recorded our second album, the band had really begun to find its feet and we had more than enough material to draw upon in order to keep the shows fresh and vibrant. The UK dates were mainly the usual city halls and so on but, despite being relatively small, these were fantastic places to perform in – it was in those time-honoured venues that we really began to develop the whole theatrical concept of the band's performance.

Even though all of those city-hall shows were great to play, the most memorable one on that particular tour was at Newcastle City Hall on 26 March 1971 when we recorded our live adaptation of Mussorgsky's *Pictures at an Exhibition*. Keith played the opening 'Promenade' section on an old Harrison & Harrison organ permanently installed above the stage in the hall.

Mussorgsky wrote the work in 1874 after seeing the paintings of his recently deceased friend Victor Hartmann at an exhibition and at his friend's home. In the very early days of

Emerson Lake & Palmer, Keith suggested that we could do our own version live and both Carl and I really liked the idea. It quickly became one of the signatures of our live performances but we had never recorded it in the studio. A film of our performance of 'Pictures at an Exhibition' at the Lyceum in London in November 1970 had been released but it was shockingly bad, both in terms of the filming and sound quality, and we wanted to redress the balance by releasing a proper live recording that would capture the energy of the band.

There was some talk of releasing the Newcastle City Hall recording as Emerson, Lake & Palmer's second album, but the record company was not convinced that an interpretation of a whole classical suite was going to sell, despite how it had gone down in our live performances. The idea was shelved for the time being, but after the success of the second album and tour, it was released in November 1971, reaching number three in the UK album charts. As well as 'Pictures', the album included the live encore of 'Nutrocker', inspired by Kim Fowley's version of the march from Tchaikovsky's ballet, *The Nutcracker*. William Neal, who created the *Tarkus* cover, did another great one for *Pictures at an Exhibition*, relating the idea of a gallery of paintings, blank on the outside but with the revealed artworks inside the gatefold.

The success of our adaptation helped tear down the walls of prejudice and bigotry that had until then helped maintain the belief that you had to be either extremely clever or upper class, or preferably both, in order to be able to enjoy classical music. It was perhaps the first time that a young rock audience had ever been offered up an honest, serious attempt at performing a piece of classical music with a rock sentiment and a rock feeling, but not in a corny, piss-taking way. It was a real attempt to make it sound good and relevant, and they appreciated it.

Following the reaction and enthusiasm shown that night by the young audience from Newcastle, and the surprising success of the record, it was clear that, at least to some small extent, the world of classical music would never be quite the same again. The sale of formal, orchestral versions of *Pictures* rose significantly after our record was a hit, and they were being bought by people who had never listened to classical music before.

Now, of course, classical music is used from everything from mobile-phone ringtones to the warm-up music for sporting events in stadiums to TV adverts. We all pretty much now take it for granted, but it wasn't like that in the early 1970s when we released *Pictures at an Exhibition*.

Despite the fact that we never actually foresaw that kind of musical liberation taking place, and that it was an accident rather than intentional – we were just playing music we wanted to play – our contribution to that has now become quite a rewarding legacy for us. Personally, I'm not really convinced that I have any great talent or that I have ever had any specific plan – I just want to entertain – but we were there in the right place and at the right time. I'm just a lucky man.

The last show on this leg of the UK tour was played in Wigan on 1 April 1971. Not so many well-known bands came to play in Wigan so none of us really knew what to expect. As is often the case in smaller towns and cities, though, the audience was fantastic. It was one of those special nights when everything just seemed to go right and the atmosphere in the room was truly electrifying.

People often ask me to name my favourite ELP performance and, of course, the ones that often spring to mind are the big festivals and more historic events. Looking back now, however, I think that some of ELP's greatest performances took place in the small city halls and theatres in the United Kingdom and the United States during the early days of the band's career.

On 15 April 1971 we boarded a plane at Heathrow and flew out to the States, giving me the chance to rekindle the love affair with the States that had started when I was in King Crimson. Of course, having witnessed the band's meteoric rise to fame in the UK and Europe, a sense of expectation was building about how we were going to be received in America.

Shortly after landing at JFK airport, we were greeted by Dee Anthony, my old friend and manager from the King Crimson era, who remained involved in the initial days of ELP. Dee bundled us all into a waiting limo and I remember the drive into Manhattan on that beautiful spring day; Dee pulled his old trick out of the hat and arranged for WNEW, a major radio station in New York, to play 'Lucky Man' as we drove across the Brooklyn Bridge on our way into the city. It is hard to imagine a more welcoming start to a tour.

The idea behind Emerson, Lake & Palmer's first US tour was that it would be a short introductory run of dates just to get the band established. The first show was to be a sort of warm-up date that took place at Thiel College, Greenville, Pennsylvania, on 21 April 1971. Although the intention was to keep this show small and low-profile, by the time we arrived there the word on the street had already spread and the demand for tickets was starting to cause a problem.

The first full show we played was on 24 April 1971 at the Eastown Theatre in Detroit. The promoter there was a remarkable man called Bob Bagaris. He was of native American descent and his personality was very calm and deliberate, rather like the stereotypical 'Red Indian' chiefs that were depicted in the cowboy films of the era.

Detroit, the home of soul and Motown, was an exciting place to be. Despite the fact that that form of music has little influence on the musical style of ELP, we all respected the players and writers who had made it so successful, and performing in Motor City had special meaning for us. The show went really well and the audience reaction was fantastic. At the time, it would have been hard to imagine that a year or two later we would be playing in the same city to audiences of 60,000 people.

The next shows on the tour were at Bill Graham's famous Fillmore East in New York, where Bill Graham himself introduced us to the audience on 1 May 1971.

The show began with 'The Barbarian' from the first ELP album and, as we played through the music, I could almost see the audience being transformed from being enthusiastically inquisitive to being absolute believers. As it was a New York gig at a legendary venue, we were nervous, but I must say that one of the great things about ELP was our innate ability to rise to the occasion. Somehow, whenever the need arose, we could always dig in and find that little extra spirit to push it over the top and that is exactly what happened that night.

We knew that if we wanted acceptance and success in the United States, then this show had to be a success and, thanks to the good grace of the people of New York, that is what happened.

The next show was at Shea's Theater in Buffalo – famous for its 'Mighty Wurlitzer' organ – on 2 May 1971, and then back to New York to perform at another landmark, Carnegie Hall, on 26 May. Apart from being a beautiful theatre, Carnegie Hall has world-class status in terms of prestige and it was an honour to perform there. I was aware of some of the great names that had stood and performed on that stage, and it was extremely humbling: Frank Sinatra, Luciano Pavarotti, the Beatles, Paul Robeson, Bob Dylan, Mark Twain, Maria Callas . . . the list goes on.

There is a classic joke about Carnegie Hall, which was told by the wife of the famous violinist Mischa Elman. One day, after a rehearsal that apparently hadn't pleased Elman, the couple were leaving Carnegie Hall by the backstage entrance when two tourists looking for the entrance approached them. Seeing his violin case, they asked him, 'How do you get to Carnegie Hall?' Without looking up and continuing on his way, Elman simply replied, 'Practice!'

The final show on the first US tour was a free concert that took place on 29 May 1971 at the Edward A. Hatch Memorial Shell in Boston. The Hatch is a beautiful outdoor venue set on grass alongside the water, and it is the traditional home of the Boston Pops. At free events, the audience is quite different from the normal ticket-buying audience that comes along specifically to see you perform. Many people simply turn up because it's free so in a sense you are often faced with a bit of a challenge to win them over, and so it was here. As we started the show, I thought, *There's something wrong – the reaction to the music is not the same.* We had to dig deep and turn up the heat during 'Tarkus'. Thank goodness all three of us were experienced enough not to allow our confidence to be shaken or diverted away from the main objective: winning over the audience with the quality of the music.

As the concert continued the audience became far more enthusiastic until, in the end, we walked off to another standing ovation. We finished the first tour on a high note, firm in the belief that the American audience was happy to embrace our sound, embedded though it was in old European traditions.

■ ■ ■

Exactly one week after performing in Boston we arrived to play at the Mehrzweckhalle in Zofingen, Switzerland, on 5 June 1971. For some reason, Switzerland always seemed to play a role in the career of ELP. *Works Volume 1* was recorded in Montreux, where we lived for a while, and the album cover for *Brain Salad Surgery* was painted by H. R. Giger, who lived and painted in Zurich.

The next show on tour was performed at the Konzerthaus in Vienna, a great place for us to perform our version of 'Pictures at an Exhibition'. We had obtained special permission for Keith to use its historic pipe organ to open the show, which was great until we came to the actual moment, only to discover that the pipe organ was tuned at a slightly different pitch than the normal 440 tuning we were used to.

Without a shadow of a doubt, the long list of world-renowned Austrian classical music composers is truly formidable, but I always wondered whether the country really connected with rock music in the same way that some other European countries did. I felt that the people there had a sort of arm's-length academic interest in modern music but somehow had not embraced the free-spirit ideal that lies at the heart of rock and roll. However, we seemed to go down very well with the audience and the show was a success.

A couple of days later, on 9 June 1971, we performed for the second time at the infamous Circus Krone in Munich, which we had now been assured would be completely safe and that there would definitely be no repeat of the water-cannon incident that brought our first visit to a premature end.

Show time arrived and we took to the stage. Everything seemed to be going okay until it came time for me to perform my acoustic set. As I started to play the J200, some heckler in the audience started shouting abuse at me and causing a disturbance. I continued on and put up with it as long as I could, but eventually I stopped playing and told him to 'be quiet' (well, perhaps I didn't use those exact words). I tried to explain to him as best I could that there were a lot of people who had paid good money to come and hear the show, and that he had no right to rob them of their enjoyment. The audience cheered but, undeterred, the heckler still continued on with his tirade until, to the delight of everyone else, the security guards finally moved in and ejected him by force. The concert continued on unimpeded and we left to a standing ovation after our 'Nutrocker' encore, but it seemed that there was some sort of a hex on Circus Kone as far as we were concerned.

The tour continued with sold-out shows in Germany and the Netherlands, with a performance at the Concertgebouw, Amsterdam, before we returned to London on 20 June to play the Theatre Royal, Drury Lane, another sell-out.

By the end of this run of European dates, we were all pretty tired and in need of a break so before setting off again to play our second tour of the USA, we decided to take a short holiday.

Whenever I get the chance, I always like to go back to Dorset where I grew up and get together with my oldest friend, Jon Petterssen. As very young lads, Jon and I used to go poaching trout together, and it was he who originally taught me how to fly fish. We have been close friends ever since. Apart from fishing, we also share a lifelong passion for music and played together for a while in the Shame during the late 1960s. Whenever Jon and I are able to meet up, we always like to go fly fishing in Dorset's chalk streams. There is something special about two old friends walking up a river together, absorbed by the enchantment and magnificence of nature.

In terms of rest and relaxation, fly fishing is not the same as sitting around on a beach. It is so absorbing that you become completely detached from the real world and all of its stresses and strains; I find that I am restored in a way that no other form of holiday could possibly hope to achieve. I suppose some of this is purely down to that old adage that a change is as good as a rest, but far more important for me is the fact that I become completely immersed in nature and become reinvigorated by all of its life-giving properties.

After spending my few precious days of rest with Jon, I returned to London on 10 July and began to prepare for the forthcoming return trip to the United States of America.

CHAPTER 7

Rocked by the King

Just before starting the second US tour in July 1971, we were due to spend a few days relaxing at the Four Seasons Hotel in San Francisco, recovering from the eight-hour time difference.

Just after I had checked in, the phone rang in my room. It was Dee Anthony calling to ask if I would like to go and see Elvis perform live on the shore of Lake Tahoe, just over the California state border with Nevada. Of course, Elvis had never performed in the UK and so this was a very special chance for me to go and see the man everyone referred to as 'The King'.

The next day we flew up to Lake Tahoe and Dee had organised wonderful log–cabins for us to stay in that were situated in the forest right beside the lake itself. I was looking out of my window, admiring the fantastic scenery, when all of a sudden there was a knock at my front door. There was Dee, standing in front of me with a huge smile on his face waving a handful of tickets he had somehow magically acquired for us to go and see Elvis perform at the casino of the Sahara Hotel that evening. I could tell by the level of Dee's excitement that this was obviously going to be something special.

I had never been to a proper casino before and, although I had images in my mind from movies, I really had no idea what to expect. We arrived a little late and were asked to go straight in and take our seats as soon as possible. As we entered the room, the first thing that struck me was that, rather than being a theatre, it was a very large dining/cabaret room filled with large, red-leather banquette couches each seating four or five people. The table in front was lit by two small lamps with shades that would be dimmed as soon the show began. As we sat down, people were being served with their after-dinner coffee and cognac, and the room was buzzing with expectation.

I immediately found the scale of the venue strange. It was hard to judge the seating capacity, but it was probably no more than 2,000 people. I suppose I had expected the King of Rock and Roll to be performing at much larger venues than those ELP were selling out at that time, but it was much smaller.

When I asked Dee about this, he looked at me with a confident smile. 'Just wait and see,' he said.

Literally moments after he had said these words, the lamps on the tables began to dim and the audience started to applaud. There were a few seconds of darkness as the tension continued to build. It almost felt as if a boxing match were about to take place and I knew that something very special was about to happen.

Over the PA system in the darkness came the first notes of the theme from the film *2001: A Space Odyssey*, 'Thus Spake Zarathustra' by Richard Strauss. If ever there was a better piece of music befitting the announcement of a king, I have yet to hear it.

As soon as the symphonic music climaxed, I heard the sound of an electric guitar together with a snare drum. It was the opening chords to 'Jailhouse Rock'. As these first chords start to play, I suddenly saw the unmistakable silhouette of Elvis with his back to the audience, his shadow being projected up on to a huge backdrop, thirty feet high. There he was: the man they call the King.

The audience exploded with excitement as a spotlight suddenly shot down and Elvis spun around singing the opening line: '*Going to a party in the county jail . . .*' Before he had even finished the first verse at least three women in front of me had fainted!

He performed only about thirty seconds of 'Jailhouse Rock' before he broke into '*Since my baby left me . . .*' Again, he only sang around thirty seconds of the song and I saw another woman pass out as he broke into the next: '*You ain't nothing but a hound dog*'.

I just could not believe what was happening. By the time Elvis had finished this spectacular opening, it was just as if a bomb had gone off. The audience was out of control, screaming, cheering, and some even looked to be pleading. There was something almost religious about the level of devotion and spirituality that was taking place. This was more than a rock concert; what I was seeing was a congregation that had come to pay homage to its god.

Elvis was clearly overjoyed by the response, and as the mayhem began to subside and settle, he went up to the microphone, half laughing and yet clearly moved. He said, 'Thank you very much, ladies and gentlemen. I'm really not worth it.'

I remember thinking to myself then, if this wasn't enough, then what on earth would I have to do in order to be worth it?

It was not until I saw Elvis perform live that I really understood why people refer to him as the King. At the time I saw him perform this particular show, it was not long after his famous black-leather comeback shows when he was almost certainly at the very top of his game.

As I watched Elvis perform on stage, I could not help but be absolutely fascinated by the way he looked. Firstly, he was six feet tall, had jet-black hair, pearl-white teeth and a suntan to die for. Everything in his wardrobe was custom designed to make him look impressive and, of course, no expense was spared on jewellery and so on.

Elvis's live show was not very long in terms of some of today's concerts, but every single song he performed was a platinum hit: just one hit after the other, after the other; it was simply relentless.

My final memory of the show was Elvis performing 'Polk Salad Annie', which was not so well known but became a staple of his concerts in the early 1970s. As the song drew towards the end, Elvis left the stage with a wave while the band kept playing round and round again on the main riff until eventually they came to a stop.

Suddenly the main florescent house lights came on and a chilling voice came over the PA with those now famous words, 'Ladies and gentlemen, Elvis has left the building.'

It really was like waking up from a beautiful dream and coming face to face with reality.

All around me there were people collecting up their belongings, women with black mascara running all down their faces, people who were confused, clearly in a state of shock, looking totally drained. I scanned the room: it was eerie – like seeing the devastation after a tornado has passed through. That is the effect that Elvis had upon people: he was such a joy to watch and to listen to that when he had gone you somehow felt totally alone and empty.

As we made our way out of the casino, we passed the Elvis merchandising stands. People were pushing and shoving just to buy items of memorabilia, some of which were limited to only one or two per person, and people started fighting each other for them.

When we eventually got outside, Dee looked at me and said, 'So, what did you think?'

There was really no need to ask because he knew as well as

I did that we had just witnessed what can only be described as a masterful performance by the King of Rock and Roll.

For a while afterwards, I must admit, I felt quite depressed because I knew that I would never be that good, but then I began to accept that, be it big or small, we all have our own contribution to make. I suppose, looking back now, things didn't work out too bad after all.

By the time we embarked on the US tour, the stature of ELP had really begun to take hold and we were now performing in far more prestigious venues all over the world. Very near the beginning of the tour, on 19 July 1971, we played the Hollywood Bowl in Los Angeles, California. I believe that this was the first ever show where large synchronised video screens were used so that everyone in the audience would be able to see the performers close up. We would no longer just be a dot in the distance to the people furthest away in the largest venues.

ELP always travelled to the venue separately. This was partly for convenience and partly because we spent so much of the day together it was good for us to create as much personal space as possible whenever the chance arose. The drive to the Hollywood Bowl that night stands out, though, because our management had arranged for three white limousines to drive us to the show. The cars drove one behind the other in procession up to the venue, and as we got closer we began to go past thousands of people making their way to the show as well. As soon as they saw the cars go past, they started to shout and scream. By the time we reached the venue, we were very nervous.

As the Hollywood Bowl is an open-air amphitheatre set against the backdrop of the Hollywood Hills, it was a most impressive sight when we walked on to the stage and looked out at the audience sitting beneath the stars. Again, as with all of these iconic venues, it was impossible to walk on to the stage without reflecting on some of the great names that had performed there before us. The show went extremely well and the band had succeeded in notching up another landmark show in its career. Keith managed to fall into the orchestra pit at one point, and it was later revealed that he had broken a rib, but that didn't stop him.

The pace of the tour started to pick up dramatically and the shows came thick and fast, so much so that after a while we began to lose touch with time and space as we passed through so many airports and cities – they all started to become a blur. The only thing that seemed constant was the show itself. Indeed, part of the skill of touring like that is to make the show as streamlined and uniform as you possibly can so that it becomes rather like a well-run circus, where everyone knows exactly what they have to do each night in order to make the show run like clockwork.

One of the very strange things I discovered was to do with the length of the show. Because of police curfews and so on, it was always important to know the length of the show, so every night our production manager would time us using a stopwatch. The incredible thing was that, even taking into account the spoken announcements and various improvisations that would obviously vary from night to night, the shows, which were approximately two-and-a-quarter hours long, were very rarely any more than thirty seconds adrift either way. Somehow, we had obviously built in an unconscious instinct for time.

Although there were continuing rumours about Dee Anthony's involvement in the mafia, there was only one time when I witnessed a direct connection between him and anyone from that world. It was during the early days of ELP, at the beginning of September 1971 during our second US tour. At the time, we were staying at the Loews Hotel in midtown Manhattan. Early one morning, the phone rang and I leaned over half asleep to pull the phone down on to the bed and lifted the receiver. There was a male voice on the other end.

'Is that Greg Lake?' he asked.

'Yes,' I said.

'I know where you're playing tonight and I am going to kill you.'

Then the receiver went down and I was listening to the dial tone.

That night ELP were scheduled to play in a place called Gaelic Park, an open-air venue over in the Bronx. It was surrounded by tall buildings and overground subway structures. It would have provided the perfect place for a sniper with a rifle.

At first, I thought that it must be a joke, but I did not recognise the voice and the man had sounded absolutely serious. I wracked my brains over and over. Why would anyone want to say that, let alone actually *do* it?

I decided to phone up Dee and tell him what had happened. His initial reaction was that it must have been one of the roadies playing a prank, but he heard me out and he soon started to suspect that the threat was genuine. Dee told me not to leave my room. He would come right over.

After about ten minutes, there was a knock on the door. I heard Dee's voice in a half-whisper saying: 'It's all right, man. It's me.'

I opened the door and Dee came in, sat down on the edge of my bed and gave me a hotel key. He had booked the adjoining room to mine and said that if anyone was to knock at my door, then I was to go through the connecting door into that room and hide in there.

He told me he was leaving but would return in a short while. He assured me that he would get this taken care of.

When the door closed behind him, I was alone once again reflecting on my fate and who could possibly have made such a menacing call.

After twenty anxious minutes, there was another knock on the door. I immediately dashed over to the door to the other room. When I opened it, there – to my absolute surprise – was Dee.

'It's okay. It's okay,' he said and ushered me back into my room. He explained that we were being visited by two gentlemen whom he thought could help.

There was another knock on my door. Dee jumped up and I heard a voice call out: 'Dee, it's Wazzle!'

Dee immediately opened the door and there stood a man who was at least six-and-a-half feet tall, towering over Dee and built like a wall. He hugged Dee as though he were a long-lost brother.

It was then that I noticed that behind him stood a short and slight gentleman dressed smartly in a long black overcoat and a matching fedora hat. He entered the room and asked me politely to sit down.

'Where did you go last night?' he asked. 'Did you get into any trouble?'

'No. There was no trouble,' I said. 'I just went to this club and then left with a girl who I had met there.'

'Where did you go then?'

'We came back here for some drinks in the bar and came up here, and she left sometime at around 2 a.m.'

'Do you still have the girl's name and telephone number?'

She had left her name and number on a piece of paper on the table so I leaned over and handed it to him.

'Okay,' he said. 'We'll be back later.'

Dee accompanied the two men as they left and they stood

in the corridor for a few moments discussing the situation. Dee then came back into the room and told me that he felt confident that they would resolve the problem.

I was now becoming increasingly fearful about what might lie in store. I asked Dee what was making him feel so confident. He just smiled and said, 'These guys have ways of dealing with problems like this. Relax. Don't worry about it.'

Dee sat in the armchair and turned on the TV. I lay on the bed. We waited for events to unfold.

An hour passed and then there was another knock at the door. Again, I rushed into the adjacent room. I could hear laughter through the connecting door and Dee saying: 'No! I don't *believe* it.' Then he came over towards the adjoining door.

'Greg,' he said. 'It's all over.'

I went back into my room and the shorter of the two men explained that the girl I had met at the nightclub was actually a hooker and that her pimp had followed us both back to the hotel. It was he who had made the threatening call.

The immediate feeling of relief I felt was quickly replaced by a feeling of dread. What did they do to the guy who made the call? Sensing my concern, the short man reached out and put his hand on my arm reassuringly. With a mischievous smile, he opened up his overcoat to reveal an armoury of hand guns and silencers that had been cleverly concealed in the lining.

'We bought him a train ticket to Atlanta,' he said. 'And told him not to come back to the city for at least two weeks.'

'Yeah,' Wazzle added. 'We had to go in and get him out of bed!'

They started laughing. They had at first paid a visit to the girl and persuaded her that it would be in her best interests to tell them everything she knew. She immediately gave them the pimp's address. Somehow, they had then managed to acquire the key to his apartment and had crept in and found him asleep. I cannot imagine the shock he must have felt when, only a couple of hours after he had made the threatening phone call to me, he was himself awoken from his slumber – and looking down the wrong end of a revolver.

After a few hugs and Italian kisses on the cheek with Dee in the corridor, both men left. Then Dee popped his head back inside the door and said; 'Enjoy the rest of the day. Forget what happened and just look forward to the show tonight.'

When the door closed, I fell back on the bed. I was drained and shaken by what had happened, and stunned by how quickly Dee's associates had managed to deal with it. It had been a bit like one of those white-knuckle rides that go all the way from sheer terror to an overwhelming sense of relief in a matter of minutes.

That night we played Gaelic Park and it was a great show – vintage early ELP where we used more Hammond organ than synths. It was at shows like this that we established our deep bond with the people of New York (and, thank goodness, I believe that a bootleg recording of that actual show still exists).

■ ■ ■

The US tour came to a close with a show at Madison Square Garden, New York, on 25 November 1971. Apart from the sheer thrill of playing at one of the world's most historic venues, on that night I learned from Dee Anthony some words of wisdom that would remain with me forever.

Shortly after arriving at the Garden, we went up on stage for the sound check before going back downstairs to the dressing room to wait for show time. This period between the sound check and the show is always a dead time so I usually try and use it to get a little extra sleep. Every time I closed my eyes, however, I could hear the noise of the audience as they began to make their way into the arena – just a few voices at first but then later on the sound changed to a kind of constant low hum being generated by the thousands of people that were gathering there.

About twenty minutes or so before show time, Dee came into the room and asked me if I would like to take a peek out at the audience from behind the curtains. At first, I wasn't that keen, but he explained to me that the Garden was a bit of an unusual building and that he thought it might be good for me to see how the audience actually looked before walking out there to perform.

In the end, I agreed, so we both set off along the corridors and made our way to the backstage area. Now the distant hum that I had heard back in the dressing room was very present as the true scale of the arena started to become apparent. We made our way up on to the stage and stood behind the curtains at the point where both sides met in the middle. Dee pulled them back just enough to see through and beckoned me to take a look. I looked through and was awestruck by what I saw.

For its capacity, Madison Square Garden is a very compact building, so in order to accommodate the 22,000 people the seats rise up in steeply raked tiers, one upon the other, towering up above and all around like a massive gladiatorial arena.

After watching my reaction, Dee smiled and said, 'Never forget, there is really only one person out there.'

When I asked him what he meant, he explained that to every single person in the audience, as they look up at the stage their perception is one of direct communication between themselves and the artist, and that has to be reciprocated. In other words: although you may look out and see all 22,000 people at once, what you are actually looking at is 22,000 different, individual people, each of whom deserves your attention.

'You are only ever playing to one person – you've got to act as if you are singing just for them,' Dee said as we turned and made our way back to the dressing room.

Throughout my entire career I have never forgotten these words of wisdom and I believe that together with Don Strike's advice about performing songs – i.e., four for the audience and one for you – this ranks as the best piece of advice I ever received during my fifty-year career.

The success of the US tour was matched by sales, with both *Tarkus* and *Pictures at an Exhibition* reaching the top ten of the Billboard 200 album charts. We returned to the UK to finish off the year with a short tour during which we played twenty shows in just eleven days.

We had been looking for somewhere special to perform in London during this tour and our first choice was the Royal Albert Hall. However, some years earlier during his days with the Nice, Keith had been banned from playing there after he burned the American flag on stage in protest against the war in Vietnam. As a result, our final appearances on that tour were six shows that took place on 13, 14 and 15 December 1971 at the more intimate Pavilion Theatre, which later became part of the Trocadero entertainment complex in Piccadilly Circus. It was Carl's idea to play there. The Pavilion was an old cinema – only a 1,000-seater – and hadn't been used for a live show since before the Second World War. Maybe because it was an old theatre and cinema, Carl surprised us by launching into the Nice's 'America' from *West Side Story* for the finale, before diverting into 'Rondo'.

By then, we had already started to record the fourth ELP album.

CHAPTER 8

Trilogy

I am often asked to choose my favourite ELP album, and I find it difficult to answer. If I were forced to choose, however, it would have to be *Trilogy*. This record was made at a time when the band was on fire. By the time we started recording at Advision Studios at the end of 1971, we had been together for long enough and played enough shows to have found our own distinctive musical identity, and at the same time music technology was advancing. We also completely trusted each other as musicians, both in the studio and in live performance. The stars were aligned.

The album is less dark and difficult than our previous albums but it has a strange, beautiful quality about it that is unique. I don't know of another album that sounds like it.

There were two important factors that influenced our thinking at the time. The first was our desire to create original music that had not been heard before. People have long since used the term 'progressive' to try and define our music, but as I said about King Crimson, this was never a term we used ourselves. We were just driven to achieve the highest possible standards for ourselves.

The second factor was the emerging technology. When we started work on *Trilogy*, tape machines had just moved up from sixteen to twenty-four tracks, and it was soon possible to synchronise – or 'slave' – two machines together to enable forty-eight-track recording. We no longer ran short of tracks or needed to bounce tracks together. Above all, we now had the freedom to experiment with overdubs and this allowed us to orchestrate our recordings in a way that had never been possible before.

Another crucial technological development at that time was the upgrading of the Moog synthesiser. It now had the capacity to perform in a polyphonic mode rather than simply a monophonic one. This meant that multiple notes could be played simultaneously rather than just one single note at a time.

We also felt we no longer had to prove anything. *Tarkus*, the live album *Pictures at an Exhibition* and the tours to Europe and the United States had shown that we weren't only as good as our first album. This confidence allowed us to take risks and venture deeper into our ambitions to create a visionary record.

I was often amazed by the depth of hatred some critics felt for this record. For them, *Trilogy* was pretentious and pompous.

And it wasn't enough simply to dislike the band or find the record boring. They were compelled to produce pages of vitriolic ranting. ELP seemed to have a special knack when it came to infuriating music critics to a point where they lost self-control.

Most bands had drawn on the influence of American music such as the blues, soul and gospel. Because we took inspiration from a European tradition instead, some music critics interpreted this as an attempt by us to look highbrow, to show off. This was definitely not part of our thinking. Both Keith and I were fans of American music in all of its forms (including country and western, in my case) but this territory had been visited far too often. We felt that it was time for a change and simply drew on music that we also liked.

It is interesting to note that ambitious, European-influenced music has so far been ignored by the Rock and Roll Hall of Fame. I honestly don't think anyone can deny the impact this form of music has had on the rock culture of the USA. A real museum should reflect history, and not be run like a radio station that chooses its playlist based on current local popularity or some programmer's own taste.

It's not just about personal or career recognition. My frustration is more to do with the huge part that Americans have played in nurturing this form of music, from industry legends such as Ahmet Ertegün, Dee Anthony, Frank Barsalona and Bill Graham to the millions of fans of ELP, King Crimson and other so-called progressive bands throughout the USA.

In fact, in the case of Emerson, Lake & Palmer, we spent so much time touring the States that people in the UK often mistakenly believed we were actually American!

Trilogy was released on 6 July 1972 in the UK and reached number two, and it went on to be our biggest-selling studio album in the United States, peaking at number five. The single 'From the Beginning', my acoustic folk song in the tradition of 'Lucky Man', was a Billboard top-forty hit and became a very strong airplay track in the United States. Like 'Lucky Man', it features a great Moog section from Keith and drums from Carl, so it was very much a band song rather than a solo by me.

The European influence and the dynamic possibilities it gave us were a key element of ELP's popularity with the general public. One moment our music could be intense, powerful and ferocious and the next it could be beautiful and gentle. The title track starts off as a wistful piano ballad but explodes into the three of us blasting in unison, while 'Living Sin' grows into a strong, earthy and animalistic song.

Keith and Carl were happy for me to play the guitar on the tracks in principle but, when I did, there was no bass. Keith tried to add bass with foot pedals but it wasn't the same and our sound was diminished by the lack of a proper bass part. As a result, I had limited opportunities to play guitar on these songs but this enabled Keith to fully explore the synths and new technology to find different colours and instrumentation, as he did on the opening track, 'The Endless Enigma', and 'Abaddon's Bolero'. European music is simply more rich, complex and colourful than the blues, which sticks to a rigid, repetitive sound. Guitar and vocals, that's the sound of the blues; European music is the sound of a 100-piece orchestra, a French horn section, a string quartet, a choir and harps.

This is not to say that we did not share American influences, and the two final tracks on the album show that clearly. 'The Sheriff' is obviously inspired by the Wild West, in terms of both the music and my lyrics. There was usually a bit of fun and humour on an ELP record – 'Jeremy Bender' and 'Are You Ready Eddy?', for instance – which didn't really suit the press stereotype of us as pretentious, and 'The Sheriff' was light-hearted. It clip-clops along as it tells the tale of the sheriff's pursuit of Big Kid Josie. We also turned to Aaron Copland's classical/country 'Hoedown', from his ballet score for *Rodeo*, but there the scope and scale were European.

In fact, the European approach gave us so much space and freedom we overdosed on overdubs. When we came to perform *Trilogy* live, it was difficult to replicate what we had done in the studio. This is why a number of tracks on *Trilogy*, such as 'Abaddon's Bolero' and 'The Endless Enigma', were rarely performed live. I lost count of how many overdubs we put on 'Abaddon's Bolero', and in order to try and recreate it live I had to add to Keith's keyboards by playing a Moog and a Mellotron, but it didn't really work. We decided that on the next album we made, we would make sure that we could perform it live.

■ ■ ■

With the recording of *Trilogy* completed early in 1972, our third tour of the United States commenced in March 1972. By this time ELP was fast becoming a very successful arena-selling act – the stage show was getting even more theatrical, with innovative lighting and pyrotechnics, and Carl's drum kit seemed to be getting bigger and bigger. So high was the demand for tickets that we would often find ourselves playing two separate arenas back to back on consecutive nights in the same area, as happened when we began this leg of the tour on 22 March at Long Beach Arena, California, followed on the 23rd by the Civic Auditorium in nearby Santa Monica.

Every time we would sell out an arena, Dee's face would light up with his incredible Italian smile and he would quote this old saying that had apparently come from his early days managing Tony Bennett: 'When you're hot, you're hot and when you're not, you're not!'

At the time, I was never quite sure what message this was really meant to convey other than perhaps one of gratitude and acceptance of the fact that, no matter how much we would like to think we control all the events that make up our lives, more often than not it is destiny that determines our fate.

Later on, however, I did come to discover that there was a very precious little pearl of wisdom contained in this expression: this was the fact that many artists go through various stages in their careers – times when they are particularly popular and times when they are not – and the advice is basically that, when you are going through a low point in your career, it is far better simply to accept it with good grace, keep your head down and work hard until things improve. It's no good trying to pretend that you are on fire and at the top of your game when the whole world thinks that you are not.

By this time, we were no longer playing 'The Barbarian', but launching into the shows with 'Hoedown'. 'Take a Pebble' and 'Lucky Man' from the first album were still regular features, though, alongside 'Pictures', 'Tarkus', 'Rondo' and material from the new album.

One of the most memorable shows we performed on this tour of the USA was the Mar y Sol Festival on 2 April 1972 in Vega Baja, Puerto Rico. Along with ELP, the festival featured the Allman Brothers, the Mahavishnu Orchestra with John McLaughlin, B. B. King, the Faces and many others.

My first recollection of this festival was landing at the airport in Puerto Rico and feeling the incredible intensity of the tropical sun as we disembarked from the plane. As they opened the cabin doors, the first blast of heat almost took my breath away. It was so strange to step down on to the runway and feel the soft tarmac beginning to melt gently as it gave way beneath my feet. This was the first time I really understood just how easy it would be for someone to die from exposure to that type of intense sunshine.

After a short journey by car, we reached the hotel where we would be staying during our performance at the festival.

Immediately upon walking into the tropical waterfall-themed lobby, it was clear that the entire hotel had been taken over by the festival promoters in order to accommodate all of the artists that were performing there. It felt almost as if we had just been transported into one of those dreadful Elvis films made in Hawaii.

We had endured a really long day travelling all the way down from New York, so by the time we had finished checking in we decided that, rather than going to join all the revellers down in the Tiki lounge, we would probably be better off just going to our rooms and preparing for the following day, when we were due to perform.

We spent most of the next day just lounging around the hotel and waiting for our departure slot to be called. We were originally supposed to go on stage to perform at eight o'clock in the evening but, as with most festivals, it was anyone's guess as to what would actually happen.

All through the day, helicopters were flying in and out of the hotel grounds, shuttling artists to and from the festival. It almost began to feel like one of those evacuation scenes from the war in Vietnam, with everyone scrambling to get on the chopper and then all the dust and leaves blowing as it took off. The whole thing would happen in reverse as the acts arrived back after performing.

Throughout the day, we would have periodical meetings in Dee's room to see if there were any updates regarding our departure time but, as the day progressed, it became clear to us that there were some quite serious problems occurring behind the scenes.

I believe that for one reason or another the original promoter had gone bust and the whole festival had now been taken over by a completely new promoter. Fleetwood Mac and a couple of other bands had dropped out. Later in the festival, Black Sabbath also failed to appear solely because there were not enough helicopters to get them to the site in time to perform.

As always, Dee made light of the situation and just kept smiling throughout. Eventually, as the day passed, it also became clear that our performance time was being put back later and later. First, it was moved to nine-thirty, and then to eleven o'clock. At this point we all began to wonder if we would actually get to play at all.

Once again Dee went off to meet with the promoters and eventually came back and told us that we now had a firm departure time. We would fly out at midnight and start to perform at 1 a.m. We were obviously quite stunned to hear that we would be going on so late, but Dee assured us that everything would be okay and that we should just go on and do a great show. Finally, the time came for us to depart and we gathered in the garden room waiting for the helicopters to land.

After a few minutes, the lights from the choppers appeared above the hotel and they began to descend into the grounds, first one, then two, and then a third landed all incredibly close together. After the incoming passengers had cleared, we were directed to keep our heads down and run over to get on board the helicopters. As soon as we were all aboard, we took off and were on our way to the festival site. On our way over, I asked the pilot about his job and how long he had been flying helicopters and he told me that he had recently finished his career in the US Army as a medevac pilot with the Eagle Dustoff unit in Vietnam. Little did I know that he was about to demonstrate his phenomenal acrobatic flying capabilities just a few moments later when we plunged out of the sky like a stone to land only a matter of yards behind the stage area where we were about to perform.

The whole thing reminded me of when King Crimson played the Palm Beach Festival back in 1969 and the comparisons were about to get stronger. As we disembarked, I noticed there was a group of people waiting to board the choppers we had just arrived in, and from the corner of my eye I saw that there were a few people carrying a stretcher. At first I thought that someone had perhaps been taken ill – like the man who had been bitten by a rattlesnake at Palm Beach – but this was worse. I noticed that the head of the body lying on the stretcher was completely covered by a blanket.

As soon as we were clear of the landing ground, I asked the backstage manager what had happened and he explained that a young boy had apparently been found dead with his throat cut. He suspected that it was some drug deal that had gone wrong.

We were then taken to a couple of mobile dressing-room trailers where we could rest up until it was time for us to perform. As always, I took a little walk over to the backstage area just to say hello to the road crew and check that everyone was in good shape and ready for the show. As soon as I arrived, one of the crew came over to me looking quite shaken and told me that it was absolute chaos and that someone had apparently just killed a rattlesnake right beneath the stage. Clearly this was not turning out to be one of those 'peace and love' events we had come to know in recent years but more of a horror film where God knows what is going to happen next.

Show time eventually came and we went out on stage to perform. As we began to play, I could immediately feel this incredible heat running right down the left side of my body. I didn't have time to check it out at first and continued playing, but as the seconds passed it just grew hotter and hotter. Eventually I glanced to my left to see that there was smoke starting to rise from the sleeve of my velvet jacket. Apparently some lunatic had erected a massive, high-powered, military searchlight on the left-hand side of the stage, which projected a sharp focus beam right at me. The sheer power of this lamp at such a close range was enough to start a fire, and that was exactly what had happened to the sleeve of my jacket. I screamed at the crew to turn it off and, mercifully, someone eventually saw what was happening and shut it down.

The Mar y Sol festival was recorded live and a record featuring excerpts from some of the live sets, including ours, was released later in 1972. Many years later, we found the entire sixteen-track tapes of our set, which included 'Tarkus' and 'Pictures at an Exhibition', and released it as a live album. The Mar y Sol Festival may have been a bit of a disaster, and an arrest warrant was apparently issued for the promoter, but we still performed at our best despite my clothing being set on fire.

Mar y Sol wasn't to be the last of festival fiascos that ELP were to experience. In the meantime, the final show on the North American leg of the tour was performed on 28 April 1972 at the Forum in Montreal. ELP were always treated like family by the people of Montreal and even to this day, when I visit there and stop by the Forum to see another artist performing, the union stagehands all stop to shake my hand and exchange memories of some of the great shows we have all played together.

After departing Montreal, we embarked on a short run of European dates in Germany, Italy, Denmark, Switzerland and Austria, which ran from 4 June through to 27 June 1972, and returned to the United States to appear together with Rod Stewart and the Faces, Humble Pie, J. Geils, and Three Dog Night at the Pocono International Raceway Festival in Pennsylvania on 8–9 July 1972.

Some people have referred to the Pocono International Raceway Festival as another Woodstock-type event, but if ever the word fiasco could be applied to a rock concert, this would definitely be the one. Security consisted of 300 hired hands, and 65 people from the Lackawanna County drug council were there, too, to deal with people who had adverse drug reactions, i.e. bad trips. In preparation for the worst, a field hospital was staffed by six physicians and eight fully trained nurses.

On 9 July, it had apparently rained on and off throughout the day and by the time we walked out on stage to perform, we were greeted by the sight of 200,000 people sitting in one huge field of mud. It was another event where the best way to describe the scene was 'truly biblical', but not in a good way: it looked like the belated eleventh Plague of Egypt.

I remember the promoters had commandeered a small Holiday Inn near to the festival site to act as dressing rooms for the bands who were about to perform.

As each band was called, some four-wheel-drive vehicles would be sent around to transport the band through the mud to the backstage area. They would literally be dropped off right at the bottom of the stairs that led up to the stage. In an attempt to avoid the delays and overruns that had hit other festivals, two stages were set up at this festival so that as one band performed the other would be making ready and setting up their equipment.

ELP had a couple of interconnecting rooms back at the Holiday Inn, where we sat waiting for our turn to go on. Every so often the phone would ring and we would be updated regarding the progress of the show and the time when we would likely be called.

Once again, the phone rang and Dee picked up the call. This time the organisers seemed to be discussing the weather as they had just received a forecast that, in a little over two hours' time, a fog would descend upon the entire festival site. The prediction was that this fog would be so dense that you would literally not be able to see your hand in front of your face.

Rod Stewart and the Faces were supposed to be the last act to perform, and ELP were scheduled to go on just before them. As soon as Dee received the news about the weather, he became extremely alert and told everyone to move fast and get on stage as soon as we possibly could. Dee was clearly aware of the implications once the fog had descended: in all probability, any act caught out by the fog would either be cancelled or they would have to return the following day to perform.

Dee was an extremely bright manager and I am sure he was already sensing that Rod and the Faces manager would also be aware of the situation: even though ELP were booked to go on first, there was more than a strong possibility that a race would develop between the two acts to try and get on stage as soon as they possibly could.

Within a couple of minutes, the four-wheel-drive trucks had arrived to pick us up and we were on our way to the backstage area. As we were bouncing through the mud, Dee explained that as soon as we reached the stage we should immediately go up and start playing, and not to waste any time at all sound checking and so on.

The moment we drew up at the stage, we were bundled up the steps and literally pushed out onstage behind the equipment. Dee had also come up on to the stage with us, just to make sure that everything started up as fast as it possibly could.

As always, there were a few moments just before we started to play when the road crew made their final checks to make sure everything was as it should be. Just as this was happening, I glanced down over the back of the stage and saw more vehicles arriving.

The next thing I heard was Dee's voice calling out for us to start playing and, just as he said these words, I saw the doors of the vehicles suddenly swing open and Rod and the Faces falling out in a big heap, face-down into the mud. They had obviously been enjoying a few light beverages before their call to duty and by the time they arrived they were clearly the worse for wear.

Simultaneously, the spotlights hit the stage and Keith opened up with the Moog and the ELP show began. Even though ELP were an extremely loud band, I could still detect some noisy commotion going on just behind the equipment. I was later told that the Faces manager had come on to the ELP stage to try and pull the power. Dee's version of what happened involved him hitting the manager and knocking him right off the back of the stage.

Apparently when this was happening, Rod had got up on the number-two stage and was trying to start the Faces show off by himself. Luckily for us, the PA and lights were already being used on our stage and eventually Rod was forced to climb back down and allow ELP to continue their show.

At the end of the performance, I looked out at the audience as we took our bow and could only see only ten or twenty feet into the crowd. The fog had now arrived, just as the organisers said it would, and visibility was fast closing in on zero. I am not sure whether Rod and the Faces ever did get to perform, but we were glad to have done the show and also very proud of Dee Anthony for everything he did to look after us.

Sadly, this was the end of Dee Anthony managing ELP in North America – he stopped after our shows in 1972. He was not only a great friend but was also a world-class manager who taught me so much about the United States and about being a performer. I will always miss him. May his soul rest in peace.

CHAPTER 9

The Rising Sun

We had all seen the reaction the Beatles had received when they played in Japan in 1966, and even then it was clear that the Japanese public was fast developing an appetite for Western rock music. Whether or not ELP would enjoy a similar reaction in July 1972 was, of course, a completely different matter so for us it really was an adventure into the unknown.

Since the early 1970s, Japan has opened up and become far more Westernised, but back then Japan's cultural identity still seemed to be defined by stereotypes that pointed to a strongly male-dominated society. On the street, you would often see ladies dressed in formal kimonos walking along behind their husbands in a very demure way, maintaining a respectful distance.

I will always remember a story that was told to me by one

of the ELP road crew about an incident involving a young Japanese female production assistant who had apparently been asked to organise some hamburgers for the crew's lunch.

The road crew had asked this young lady if it would be possible get some burgers from the then newly established McDonald's in Tokyo. Although this young woman had previously been very helpful, on this particular occasion she seemed strangely reluctant. The ELP production manager asked her if there was a problem, but she was unable to explain and eventually left to pick up the burgers.

Almost two hours passed before she eventually returned, by which time everyone was dying of hunger. When asked why she had taken so long, a Japanese translator explained that when the woman had gone to McDonald's she had apparently been served by a male assistant who, upon hearing her request for thirty hamburgers, immediately sent her to the back of the queue. She was told to wait there until he was ready to serve her.

The translator then went on to explain how, in order for her to eventually get served, the production assistant had to express to the male manager how sorry she was for making such an unreasonable request and that she realised that she was basically a stupid girl and that she would be eternally grateful for his generous indulgence.

In other words, in order to get served some hamburgers she had had to demean herself in front of him. She had known this would happen, which was why she was so reluctant to go in the first place.

I very much like and respect the Japanese people but even today there is no question that it does take a little while for a Western person to tune in and fully appreciate how different our two cultures actually are. Honour, politeness, simplicity and a respect for social order are all viewed through a very different prism to the way we view things in the West.

So there we were, Emerson, Lake & Palmer, about to embark on the trip of a lifetime to perform in a country which for us back then still conjured up images of samurai warlords, the Second World War and the atomic bomb. I'm not sure that any of us really knew what to expect from Japan, but I am sure we had a suspicion we would receive a warm welcome if only because we had been booked to perform in huge stadium venues.

Ever since the very early days, ELP's stage production was relatively large in scale, and since we wanted to make sure that the shows in Japan were every bit as good as any we played in the rest of the world, we insisted on taking all of our own equipment. This, of course, proved to be extremely expensive.

At the time, someone made a joke about the fact that it would probably be cheaper to buy our own aeroplane rather than fly everything there by commercial airlines. A few days later, some bright spark in the office managed to organise a deal with JAL for us to charter our own jet that would take the whole show there and back, and so luckily this resolved the problem. There would only be a dozen or so people on board – the band, management and some of the crew – but the plane would be far from empty: we were transporting about seven or eight tons of equipment.

On the day we departed from Heathrow, I remember going out to the plane and photographs being taken on the aeroplane steps. The *Sunday Telegraph* had appointed a journalist, Alexander Frater, who became a leading travel writer, to accompany us for the entire Japanese tour. It was a strange feeling when we eventually got inside this huge plane to be the only passengers on board. It must also have been the first time any of us had any close contact with real Japanese culture.

I was immediately struck by the appearance of the Japanese air stewardesses and by the delicate and very ornamental food they served, which was very different from the type of food we were used to back home. Now, of course, there are Japanese restaurants and sushi bars in just about every city on the planet, but back then none of us had ever experienced Japanese cuisine in any shape or form, so it was all very new and exciting.

Due to the length of the flight, the plane was forced to stop off in Alaska on the way over to Japan for refuelling. Upon arrival in Alaska, we all took the chance to stretch our legs and take a bit of a walk around the airport terminal, and I was awestruck at suddenly being confronted by a massive stuffed polar bear that was standing right in the middle of the departure lounge. This bear stood well over seven feet tall and it was immediately apparent to me how little chance anyone would stand if they were attacked by such an immensely powerful animal.

After reboarding, we continued on with the flight and eventually reached our destination, Narita International Airport in Tokyo. After clearing Japanese customs and its scrupulously efficient and overly suspicious officers, we were eventually escorted towards the arrivals lounge.

As the two large, frosted-glass doors parted, we were completely shocked by the deafening screams and pandemonium that instantly erupted among the hundreds of fans that had gathered there, waiting for us to emerge. In order to reach the waiting cars, we realised that we would need to somehow make our way through the frenzied crowd and that this was fast developing into a potentially dangerous situation.

Three or four people from the local promoter's office suddenly appeared out of the crowd and assured us that if we all stuck together everything would be okay. They then proceeded to link their arms in ours and attempted to frogmarch us through the crowd towards the exit doors.

Almost immediately I could feel my hair being pulled and people tearing at my clothes, and for a moment the situation became really quite unnerving. Keith had a silver bracelet snatched from his wrist during the mayhem, and I think he lost a ring as well. It was not a pleasant experience. Eventually the police waded in and managed to hold back the crowd long enough for us to reach the waiting cars and we sped off to the hotel.

On the first night in Tokyo, we didn't get much sleep at all due to the screaming girls that were camped en masse in the street outside the hotel. On the following day, the police erected barriers across the road and we were moved to rooms at the rear of the hotel, where at last we managed to get the rest we so badly needed after the long-haul flight. For the next couple of days, we did quite a lot of tourist stuff, sightseeing and visiting temples, as well as doing some press interviews, which was great because it gave us the chance to recover from the brutal time change.

Our first concert in Japan was at Kourakuen Kyujyo Suidoubashi, a sports stadium in Tokyo, on Saturday 22 July 1972.

The day of the show had at last arrived and the whole event seemed to be charged with an almost unbearably high level of expectation. In my experience, at a moment like that, while everything in your own mind is telling you to remain calm and just play the best show you possibly can, at the same time every hand you shake and your own is trembling, and everyone around you is basically on the verge of panicking, not least of all the police.

Although the stadium had witnessed capacity audiences for sporting events such as baseball, the organisers and the police were now being confronted by an entirely different level of crowd enthusiasm, which even at the beginning had the potential to slip out of control very quickly.

The day before the show, we had a production meeting in the hotel to discuss set lists and all of the other elements involved in the performance, and Keith pulled out this huge samurai sword from behind his back and laughed like hell. We realised in an instant what he had in mind. By that point, Keith was well known for pulling out a pair of daggers during our performances of 'Rondo', and it had become something of a trademark crowd pleaser. This time, however, instead of the daggers the Japanese Samurai sword would be drawn in their place. Not only was this a cool idea, but it was also a great way for us to pay our own small tribute to Japanese culture. We were quite sure that the Japanese audience would enjoy that little twist.

The next day, on the drive from the hotel, everyone in the car was extremely quiet and, as we approached the outer ring road of the stadium, we could already hear the noise of the audience from inside. As the cars entered the stadium through the tunnels, the audience noise became so deafening we could not even hear ourselves think. The cars eventually pulled up at the rear of the stage, which had been erected at the dead centre of the baseball field. We all jumped out of the cars and proceeded directly up on to the stage where we stood waiting in the wings for the word go.

Tokyo was extremely humid, and even at night the temperatures remained very high, which added to the intense atmosphere.

As we stood waiting in the wings we all got dressed into

three perfectly matching white silk kimonos, embroidered with our individual names across the back of each one.

At last, the moment had arrived, the spotlights fired up and, as we walked out on stage, we heard a Japanese voice over the PA calling our names, which caused what I can only describe as an earth-shaking reception. The Japanese character is usually portrayed as polite and restrained, but we were seeing a whole other side.

The noise level was simply stupendous as we stood there with our backs to the audience proudly displaying our names across the back of our kimonos.

After a few seconds, we quickly went backstage, dropped off the kimonos, picked up our instruments and started to play.

At some point during the show, it started to rain, quite gently at first but then getting worse and worse right up until the end of the show, by which time it had transformed itself into a mini typhoon. It didn't seem to dampen the crowd's enthusiasm. Everything we played that night brought about an instant standing ovation.

The last thing I can remember from the concert is the incredible noise that went up when Keith pulled out the samurai sword and stuck it into the keys of his Hammond organ. Somehow he had managed to get the sword to remain wedged in between the keys and it swayed back and forth as the organ wailed away in agony and the typhoon raged. Quite a poetic scene.

After the show, we were taken to this extraordinary fish restaurant for dinner and it was really quite unlike anything we had ever seen before. The restaurant was situated down by the harbour front and was set up under canvas in the open air. Although the storm had passed, the wind was still quite strong and blew the hanging light bulbs back and forth as the smoke from the chefs' fires swirled all around.

We were all sitting at a wooden bar that surrounded a very large square marble structure that rose up in the middle to form a sort of pyramid. It rather resembled a gigantic version of one of those fish display counters you sometimes get at very high-end supermarkets. Every type of fish and crustacean imaginable was out on display to form this spectacular centrepiece for everyone to admire and eventually make their selection from.

Right at the very top of this marble pyramid structure sat three chefs, appropriately dressed in kimonos and matching white bandanas. Each of the chefs cooked over his own charcoal fire and was equipped with a wooden paddle. When a customer selected a fish, the chef would use the paddle to reach down and deftly pick up the fish and retrieve it for preparation. He would then skilfully gut and wash the fish before skewering it, salting it and finally roasting it over the glowing embers.

When the fish was finally ready to eat, the chef would place it back on the wooden paddle and slide it right onto the awaiting plate in front of the customer.

I can still call to mind the scene now, watching the light bulbs dance in the swirling smoke while the smell of ocean-fresh fish roasted over charcoal permeated the warm sea air.

Sunday 23 July was a day off and we once again enjoyed the unusual sights of what to us was such a strange culture, visiting shrines and doing a little shopping as well. The two things that everybody seemed to be interested in at the time were the newly emerging Sony hi-fi products and the wonderful Japanese cultured pearls.

The concert on Monday 24 July at the Koshien Stadium, another baseball park, this time in the city of Osaka, was to be another one of those life-changing experiences that no one ever expects to happen. Apart from the sheer scale of the event, just the fact of being where we were at that moment in time was an unbelievable privilege for people like ourselves who, without the blessing of music, would probably never have travelled far beyond the perimeters of our own home towns. And yet here we were, making our way to perform at another one of Japan's great sporting stadiums.

The run-up to the event was pretty much scripted in the same way as it had been in Tokyo. The cars drove into the stadium, right on to the pitch, and we climbed on the stage and started to play. The audience reaction in Osaka seemed even more extraordinary – every song that we played just drove the audience to a higher pitch of frenzy – but the crowd were being held back some way from the stage.

As we came towards the end of the show, I could see some of the fences starting to give way and people were beginning to run on to the field to get closer to us. At first, the riot police were able to hold them back and control the situation, but after a while more and more people broke through until it became an avalanche of bodies just pouring all over the pitch and heading towards the stage.

As all of this started to take place, Keith and I left the stage while Carl was beginning his drum solo in 'Rondo'. Suddenly I was grabbed by one of the police guards, dragged down the stairs and bundled into a police car waiting behind the stage. Keith followed a few seconds later and the car sped off across the field, heading for the exit tunnel. God only knows what would have happened if the crowd had reached the vehicles before we reached the tunnel. It hardly bears thinking about.

Within a few seconds, we were driving around the perimeter of the stadium, thinking that Carl had got out as well. However, we suddenly realised that we could hear Carl's drums thrashing away: he was still playing his drum solo inside the stadium. He was obviously unaware that we had departed and the last thing we heard was his cue for us to come back on being played over and over again.

There's a funny account of this in Keith's autobiography, in which he describes us winding down the car windows when we were two miles down the freeway, and I said, 'You know he's a fucking good drummer. Listen to that! No PA, we're two miles away and you can still hear the fucker!'

Later on, we were relaxing in a Jacuzzi, but Carl still hadn't turned up. I wondered what had happened to him.

'Dunno,' said Keith. 'He's probably just about to take his T-shirt off during the gong-smashing bit.'

Another hour later, we were still relaxing when Carl threw open the doors.

'You bastards! I kept giving the cue for you to come back on and here you are frothing away in . . . in a fuckin' Jacuzzi!'

There is no question about the fact that these two shows created a historic landmark in the career of ELP. It's a shame that we never went back to Japan when we were in our prime. It was probably time constraints and the enormous costs of getting our equipment there and back that stopped us returning as a band in the 1970s.

A few days after the show in Osaka, we all flew back to the United States to embark on our fourth tour of the country, kicking off in California on 27 July 1972 at the Civic Auditorium, San Francisco, and then continuing right throughout the States until the end of August. The Far East had its effect on Keith and Carl – Keith was wearing a red kimono and Carl was in a karate outfit.

After a short summer break, we then embarked on another tour of the UK, the highlight of which was undoubtedly our performance at the Oval cricket ground in London on 30 September 1972 to thank all of our dedicated UK fans for our recent *Melody Maker* poll awards success. We had won seven awards – everything from top group to top composers, with Carl winning best drummer, Keith winning best keyboardist and me taking home the best producer award.

Playing the Oval was quite a strange experience because this iconic venue has always been associated with the very English game of cricket and in particular the 'Ashes' against Australia. It is rather as if a band today were to suddenly turn up and perform a concert at Wimbledon's Centre Court. Anyway, play it we did to a crowd of 18,000 people, with Genesis and Wishbone Ash among the support acts. We had our two huge armadillo tanks, inspired by the cover of *Tarkus*, roaring and belching smoke at the sides of the stage, and played 'Tarkus', 'Pictures at an Exhibition', 'Hoedown' and 'Lucky Man' among others.

The MC/announcer that night was a man who later became a great friend: Alan 'Fluff' Freeman, the top Radio 1 disc jockey who over the years became a British institution. Apart from being a big fan of Emerson, Lake & Palmer, Alan was also a walking encyclopaedia on the subject of opera. It was Alan who first opened my eyes to that wonderful art form.

CHAPTER 10

Salad Days

The year 1972 was undoubtedly a landmark for ELP – it was one the most creative and positive periods in the band's entire history. We had come of age musically and had also managed to establish our presence at the very cutting edge of the emerging music technology.

After the success of *Trilogy* and all of the accolades the band had received during that period, we began to realise, perhaps for the first time, that there was a slight sense of having a reputation to live up to and, of course, having to face up to that same old question, 'Are you going to be as good as your last hit record?'

For a while, Keith was talking about doing his own solo project but his enthusiasm waned and he was still committed to the band. Perhaps the only dark cloud on the horizon was the realisation that in future we would need to be more careful about the amount of overdubbing we did on our records. Although we had a great deal of confidence in our own writing and creative abilities, no matter how good we were as a live band, the whole *Trilogy* album remained extremely difficult to replicate in a live performance.

We had come to realise that, unless we intended carrying around a whole team of backing musicians to replicate all of the parts on a record, we had to change our recording techniques. It may sound obvious to anyone reading this now, but at the time multi-track recording was pretty much uncharted territory.

In the end, we came to the conclusion that if we wanted to maintain our basic, three-piece band identity, it was essential for us to be able to perform the next album live first rather than trying to figure out how to perform it all after the record had been made.

Somehow we needed to set up a situation whereby we could fully perform and demo the album live before moving into the studio. The more I thought about this whole idea of live performance, the more I began to realise that the whole essence of this record could revolve around the concept of a theatrical performance.

At around the same time, we formed our own record label called Manticore Records, which was named after the mythical beast that had also inspired the 'Manticore' section of 'Tarkus'. A manticore is often depicted with a human head, the body of a lion and a scorpion's tale – both Keith and I were born under Scorpio. The idea behind the label was not only for us to better control the production and distribution of our own records, but at the same time to also help other non-mainstream artists (just as we had been helped ourselves in previous years) to get a foot through the door. I liked working with other bands. By then I had already helped to produce Spontaneous Combustion's debut record, and we signed Stray Dog and a few other bands – including Premiata Forneria Marconi and Banco, two of the biggest acts in Italy – to Manticore Records. The truth was, though, that ELP took up almost all of our time so Manticore Records only lasted a few years.

To solve our recording issues and to push forward the broader Manticore concept – and I know this sounds horribly extravagant – we decided to buy a cinema in Fulham and convert it into a rehearsal and recording facility, which Led Zeppelin and Bad Company went on to use. We set up on the stage when we wrote our next album, and that is where the early rehearsals for *Brain Salad Surgery* took place.

We were helped in all this by our new manager, Stewart Young. He was a young accountant working with his father when we first came across him – we had gone to his firm to sort out some financial issues. When his father mentioned Emerson, Lake & Palmer, Stewart had never heard of us and thought we were a law firm. Luckily, he went to see us in concert and was amazed – and the relationship grew from there. He had no experience in the music business, but he was exactly what we needed: he had great management and financial skills and a real understanding of what we wanted to achieve and how to go about doing it.

One day we were playing live in the cinema and a lyric came to me:

Welcome back, my friends, to the show that never ends . . .

It became part of 'Karn Evil 9' and the title of our next live album.

During the time that all this was taking place, I had been meeting up with Pete Sinfield, my old writing partner from the King Crimson days. I explained to Pete some of the issues we had encountered performing the *Trilogy* album and that we were now looking to make a record that somehow contained the essence of a live theatrical performance.

In the midst of one of these discussions, I think we must have started reflecting on the whole *In the Court of the Crimson King* theatrical pageantry and noted that there could possibly be some link or loose connection between these two ideas. In any case, a few weeks later ELP set up in the new Manticore theatre and we began writing and developing some of these new ideas together.

The whole period we spent at Manticore was packed full of energy and vision for the future. We had now reached a point in our career where we knew we had the strength and the necessary resources to do something really meaningful.

Part of what had changed between 1970 and 1972 was the size and type of venues in which we were being asked to perform. Sometimes these ranged all the way from small 1,500-seat clubs right up to 20,000-seat arenas. It was proving difficult, as a small three-piece band with a basic back line of equipment, rented lights and PA, to adapt our set up to the wide range of venues.

I suggested creating a more controlled environment where we would carry our own permanent stage lighting and PA in order to maintain the same acoustics and the same type of show every single night. Everyone could immediately see the sense in this idea, so we set about designing a brand new proscenium-arch stage set that would remain constant no matter where we performed.

As the rehearsals were taking place in Fulham, the stage set itself was being constructed at Shepperton film studios, just to the west of London. All in all, this was a period of incredible and intense activity on all fronts.

The stage itself was an extremely innovative design for its time, consisting of an aluminium framework construction from which could be hung over 100 spotlights, flying monitor speakers, the PA and so on, with rooms beneath for mixing, guitar changes and so on.

The stage set became a little private world that we would take with us everywhere we performed, the idea being that the only thing that would change every night would be the audience.

Although we did experience some early teething difficulties, it very soon became a fluid operation and went on to form a basic template for other bands' future festival and large rock shows.

ELP were often criticised for running an overblown or overproduced show, but to this day I always smile when I see these huge event shows roll out their Persian carpets on stages that bask beneath their now even larger proscenium arches, and reflect on how this whole rock extravaganza production concept first began. The Persian carpets are useful because they cover the crisscross of wires over the stage, reduce slippage, absorb some of the noise so you can hear each other play and – this is the prima donna element – they make you feel more comfortable and at home on stage because they add familiarity and are softer on the feet when you are standing there performing for a couple of hours. They also help insulate you from getting an electric shock from the microphone, which happened to me on stage in 1973. And yes, my carpet really did cost $6,000.

Just prior to recording *Brain Salad Surgery*, we embarked upon our fourth European tour. We kicked off in Germany at the Ostseehalle, Kiel, on 30 March 1973, immediately followed off by the Philipshalle in Düsseldorf on 31 March. Apart from the show itself at the Philipshalle, where we introduced the audience to part of our new thirty-minute piece, 'Karn Evil 9', as well as performing 'Tarkus' and 'Pictures at an Exhibition', this was to turn out to be a momentous occasion for a completely different reason. This was the day I first met my wife Regina at a reception that had been held there for us.

The tour, called 'Get Me a Ladder', had some shaky moments when a few shows got cancelled due to bad weather, followed by a dose of very severe laryngitis, which meant that I couldn't sing, but musically we soon hit our stride. (Which was just as well as the tour was being filmed by a television crew for a documentary to be shown in the UK on Boxing Day 1973.) The tour ended on 4 May 1973 at the Velodromo Vigorelli in Milan, Italy. The locals were a literally riotous lot: famously Led Zeppelin fans had clashed with the riot police at the venue in 1971, and when our original show was cancelled twice due to the weather and my laryngitis, a crowd gathered outside our hotel and started throwing stones. Fortunately, the rescheduled show in front of 50,000 people proved to be a happy if somewhat unruly conclusion to the tour.

Although we were not so aware of it at the time, this tour was to become a significant event in the band's European career. It not only defined our success as a band with our own brand of music, but it had also confirmed that we were at the very cutting edge of live show production.

We returned home to finish working on our new songs at Manticore, and recorded the *Brain Salad Surgery* album at Advision and the Olympic Studios in Barnes. Pete Sinfield co-wrote 'Benny the Bouncer' and 'Karn Evil 9: 3rd Impression' with myself and Keith. 'Karn Evil 9', which is made up of three 'Impressions', would become regarded as one of our classic works and a favourite at our live performances. Each part had a different theme about the loss of humanity as humankind supposedly progresses, about time and travel, and about trying to get back to our original identity despite the computerisation of the world. It has the distinction of having Keith's only vocal credit on an ELP record: he provided the voice of the muse on the '2nd Impression' and ran his voice through his Moog kit to create the computerised voice in the '3rd Impression'.

Keith wrote 'Toccata', which is based on part of a piano concerto by Alberto Ginastera, and told a funny story about getting permission to adapt the work. Most of the great European composers that influenced our music were well and truly dead – so we didn't usually require permission – but Ginastera, an Argentinian, was alive and well and living in Geneva. Permission was not granted by his publishers, Boosey & Hawkes, so Keith flew off to Switzerland with Stewart Young to try and convince the composer himself to change his mind. Keith played him the music, and at the end he thought he heard Ginastera exclaim: 'Terrible!'

Luckily, it turned out that he had shouted 'Formidable!' so 'Toccata' could be included on the album. It gave Carl the chance to experiment with electronic percussion, and I think he was one of the first drummers to use it on a recording. Ginastera was willing to publicly praise an ELP version of his music and said, 'Keith Emerson has beautifully caught the mood of my piece.'

The other songs on the album were 'Still . . . You Turn Me on', a folk-style song I penned in the tradition of 'Lucky Man' and 'From the Beginning', which became an airplay hit in the States, and our version of William Blake and Hubert Parry's 'Jerusalem', which was the opening track. Carl, Keith and I were all proud of 'Jerusalem' – we loved the beauty of the melody as well as the words, and worked hard to get it right, taking two eighteen-hour sessions just to do the mixing. We thought we had done the song justice and wanted to release it as a single, but the BBC banned it from receiving airplay because they thought it was disrespectful and 'degraded' the hymn. How times have changed. Like 'Lucky Man', some people misunderstood the song – they thought I wrote the lyrics, rather than William Blake back in 1804, and believed they were somehow related to the Israel–Palestine conflict.

The album cover featured a biomechanical female skull design by the surreal Swiss artist H. R. Giger and, for the first time, the ELP logo. There was a theme throughout our music about the struggle between man and machine, so the bio-mechanical image was a perfect match. The artwork also reflected the naughty original title of the album, 'Whip Some Skull on Ya', a euphemism for fellatio, which we ended up abandoning, but the replacement title was a reference to the same thing so the cover idea didn't really need to change. However, it had to be toned down a bit to make sure the record did not get banned – there was a sort of phallus beneath the woman's mouth which was a bit too graphic and had to be turned into a shaft of light. Giger later became famous for designing the creature in Ridley Scott's *Alien*.

Brain Salad Surgery was released on 19 November 1973. It received some excellent reviews but, by now, it was obvious that some critics hated us and wasted a lot of inches insulting us personally rather than writing about the music. When we played live on stage we could hear the reaction of the audience, and we knew they loved our music. If some people love you, other people won't – that's just the way of the world. The negative critics didn't affect the sales anyway, so maybe the record-buying public thought the personal attacks were as bizarre as we did. The album reached number two in the United Kingdom and number eleven in the United States. To celebrate its release, we embarked upon our fifth North American tour on 14 November, starting at the Hollywood Sportatorium in Florida, where we opened with 'Jerusalem'.

British rock bands were making a big impression in the States at the time – you could call it a second 'British Invasion' – a rock invasion after the pop invasion of the 1960s. Our little effervescent island had produced David Bowie, Elton John, Led Zeppelin and Pink Floyd, all of whom were making an impact on both sides of the Atlantic. British music labelled as progressive was at its height, with Yes, Jethro Tull, Genesis and so on all selling records. I was often asked – I still am – what it felt like to be part of that. The truth is that we never even thought about it. We would say hello to other bands at airports and some of us had appeared on the same bills, but we never really got together – we never felt as if we were part of any sort of 'movement' and there was not some sort of British rock band union. I shared an apartment in London with Chris Squire of Yes for a while in the early days and we remained friends, but the bands didn't mix. We were not looking over our shoulder at what the likes of Yes were doing, musically or on stage, and wondering whether they were influenced by us or whether we could learn from them. All we were concerned about was ELP, and trying to make our music and performances as good as they could be.

By now the ELP stage show had begun to build into a huge amalgam of music and technology which, when viewed through the prism of a three-piece rock band, was quite impressive. By then, Carl Palmer had developed his hand-engraved revolving stainless-steel drum kit, which weighed in at four tons and kept our crew of roadies busy erecting and dismantling it at every new venue: constructing the Japanese pagoda framework and setting up the drum kit, the huge Paiste gongs and the church bell. Meanwhile, David Hardstone and IES, his innovative sound company, had developed our thirty-channel quadrophonic PA system, incorporating thirty-six-ton stacks of thirty-two speakers. The equipment took a huge logistical operation to transfer from venue to venue.

This period is remembered by many as ELP's golden era. While *Trilogy*, for me, might be the best studio album we ever made, they might well be right. During the *Brain Salad Surgery* era, we had pushed technology and stagecraft even further, and perhaps even more importantly, the band still felt like a family, all pushing together in the same direction. This combined spirit really came out during our live shows. Later on, the band started to splinter as our individual egos took centre stage and we pushed in different directions, rather than as a united force.

The tour continued to storm right across the United States until we came to the last show that was the unforgettable performance at Madison Square Garden, New York, on 17 December 1973. This was one of those shows that I still get people coming up to me and talking about to this very day. Apart from the fact that any show at the Garden is special, it was the final show on a remarkably successful tour, so we decided to pull out all the stops.

On top of this, it was also Christmas-time, which is why, towards the end of the show when we were performing 'Pictures at an Exhibition', we segued into the Christmas carol 'Silent Night', with my voice joined by the extraordinary sound of the Harlem Gospel Choir, dressed in their maroon and white robes. And then, of course, there was the artificial snow, pre-arranged to fall inside the Garden while the final verse of 'Silent Night' welcomed in the Christmas season.

It still sends shivers down my spine. It was probably the most spectacular single stage production I have ever been involved in.

The audience went crazy, but how could we add to that moment with another climax to mark the end of the show?

With Keith, of course, rising fifteen or twenty feet up into the air on a full-size grand piano, revolving around amidst smoke and flames, playing a Chopin etude.

After the performance, we were elated and exhausted.

We returned back to the UK for Christmas and for a well-deserved rest.

On 5 January 1974, Regina and I married at St James's Church in Spanish Place, George St, London W1. We have been married now for over forty years, which in the music business is, of course, quite remarkable and this, I have to say, is entirely due to her strength of character, devotion and forbearance. Without a doubt, this proved to be one of the most meaningful days of my entire life.

Just a few days after the wedding took place, ELP were back on the road again in the USA for another North American tour. As with the tour the previous year, the band were flying high and performing at the very top of their game. Every show was a sell-out and perhaps the only downside that had started to become apparent was the sheer fatigue of continually moving along at such a pace and being on duty pretty much every waking hour. If it wasn't a show or a sound check, it was a rehearsal or an interview or a planning meeting or flying to the next city. Quite often, when a day off arrived, we would all simply spend the whole day in our beds. I had always enjoyed looking around the different cities and experiencing other cultures wherever we went on tour, but by now we had started to feel like we were cogs in a machine as we went from the airport to the hotel to the venue and back to the hotel, and started the process all over again in another city on the following day.

Nevertheless, by this point in our career virtually every show had something memorable about it. The show at the Anaheim Convention Center in California on 10 February 1974 was recorded for the live album, *Welcome Back, My Friends, to the Show that Never Ends – Ladies and Gentlemen*. It resulted in surprising sales for a live triple album (it had to be six sides to include almost the entire concert), selling over 500,000 copies in the United States alone and reaching number four on the Billboard 200 charts, and peaking at number six in the United Kingdom. The album is not just a rattle through our most famous songs: it was full of the little twists and turns, improvisations and unrecorded music that would feature in a full ELP concert. There are improvised snatches of everything from the Laurel and Hardy theme tune to Joe Sullivan's 'Little Rock Getaway' to Rachmaninoff's 'First Prelude' and King Crimson's 'Epitaph' among the likes of 'Tarkus', 'Karn Evil 9', 'Take a Pebble' and 'Hoedown'.

On this particular leg of the tour, one show that still sticks in my memory was the California Jam festival at Ontario Speedway, which took place on 6 April 1974.

ELP were added late to the bill in order to help boost ticket sales. It became a record-breaking show in terms of paid tickets – supposedly over 350,000 people – and the promoters became so worried that they stopped selling tickets. Estimates vary regarding the real size of the audience that attended, and all I can tell you is that from up on stage, the audience stretched back as far as the eye could see – perhaps there were half a million or more. It had the loudest amplification system ever installed at the time, and we brought out a team from IES just to make sure our sound quality was as good as it could be. The festival also ran to schedule, which was highly unusual in those days.

On the bill that day were Deep Purple, Black Sabbath, the Eagles and numerous others. For some strange reason, the promoters had still not determined a running order for the show by the time we arrived on site. We were asked when we would prefer to go on and perform, and we said that we really didn't mind.

I think that, in the end, all the managers of the headline acts ended up drawing straws and it turned out that we were chosen to finish the show after Deep Purple's set. It seemed that some of the members of Deep Purple were not happy about their position on the bill because they had wanted to play at dusk. Whatever the reason, they apparently threw some of their equipment into the audience and, at some point towards the end of their performance, Ritchie Blackmore smashed the head of his guitar into one of the very expensive ABC movie cameras that were being used to film the event. This resulted in a huge fine, which was summarily deducted from their fee.

ELP eventually got on stage around 9 p.m., and it was freezing cold out there in the desert but we performed one of the best shows of our entire career – we were at the zenith and it went like clockwork – so it's probably just as well that Deep Purple got on and off when they did.

We returned to the UK sometime later in April to embark upon yet another UK and European tour including a four-night run of sold-out shows at the Empire Pool – which was renamed Wembley Arena – in London and two nights at the Palais des Sports in Paris. Just to give an idea of our perform-ances at that time, and how we had evolved as a live band incorporating both early and more recent songs, the Wembley set list was typical of the tour (although we often still also played 'Jeremy Bender' and 'The Sheriff'):

1. 'Hoedown'
2. 'Jerusalem'
3. 'Toccata'
4. 'Tarkus'
5. 'Benny the Bouncer'
6. Fugue from 'Take a Pebble'
7. 'Still . . . You Turn Me On'
8. 'Lucky Man'
9. Piano improvisations
10. Fugue from 'Take a Pebble'
11. 'Karn Evil 9'
12. 'Pictures at an Exhibition'
13. 'Nutrocker'

While some critics might have claimed that we were pretentious, we were not the sort of band that refused to play any music that wasn't on our latest album. Again, as Don Strike had taught me, 'Four for the audience . . .' The best performances often occur when the band are happy playing, and the audience get to hear the songs that already mean so much to them as well as some newer material.

By this point, the cities were all starting to become even more of a blur and, in truth, if we knew then what we know now we should have probably stopped touring for a while in order to refuel and re-energise the batteries. But at that time no one really had any clear idea about career pacing or the danger of what happens when an artist starts to burn out. The whole focus was simply upon the next challenge that lay ahead and how best to accomplish it, and so it was that we embarked upon what was to become the seventh ELP tour of North America.

One of the most memorable dates on this tour was the August Jam at the Charlotte Motor Speedway, North Carolina, performed on 10 August 1974.

This was another one of those open-air, Woodstock-type festival events that dominated rock music at the time, and this one featured ELP, the Allman Brothers Band, Black Oak Arkansas and numerous others. ELP had originally been booked to headline the festival but, when we arrived at the site, it was obvious that there were some arguments taking place between the Allman Brothers Band's managers and the promoter about who was supposed to be headlining the show.

Reading between the lines, I think that when the Allman Brothers Band discovered that ELP had been booked to headline, they did not feel comfortable because this show was pretty much taking place on their home turf – they were from Florida, further down the eastern seaboard. Quite why they had not discovered that we were headlining before the actual day of the show still bewilders me but they were pretty much demanding that if they were going to perform at all, then they had to be the last act of the evening.

The promoter came over to our dressing-room trailer and explained the situation. We told him that it wasn't a big deal to us and that we would be just as happy to go on and perform before the Allman Brothers. Consequently, our show time was reset for 9 p.m. that evening.

Nine o'clock arrived and we were ready and waiting to go, but there was some complication with the sound system that had come about as a result of the belated change to the running order. The set change was delayed by around forty-five minutes.

We took to the stage a little before ten o'clock and performed one of the shows of our lives. As we finished the encore of a shortened version of 'Pictures at an Exhibition', the audience just went crazy. The whole festival site was lit up by a magnificent firework display that our team had arranged. We left the stage area immediately in a helicopter and some of the fireworks screamed right past us and threatened to take out the rotor blades.

At the base, we returned to our trailers to dry up, get changed and so on, and eventually went back to say our thank yous and goodbyes to all the local dignitaries, promoters, festival crew, etc.

At around midnight, the Allman Brothers Band had for some reason still not taken to the stage so we boarded a helicopter again and took off from the festival site. As we looked down, all we could see were thousands upon thousands of people streaming away from the site on their way home, obviously thinking that the show was over.

We were later told that the Allman Brothers Band finally got on stage to perform at 2.30 in the morning!

A week later, on 17 August 1974, we were booked to play at the 24,000-capacity Roosevelt Stadium at Droyer's Point, New Jersey.

The stage where we were due to perform had been erected on the pitch at one end of the stadium, and the trucks, dressing-room trailers and other facilities were all gathered around and behind the stage. When we arrived at the stadium, it was a beautiful sunny afternoon and everything was peaceful and relaxed. We were told that the sound check was scheduled for 4.30 p.m. and went to the trailers for a rest until then. I lay in my trailer reading a book but I must have fallen asleep almost straight away because it only seemed like seconds later that someone was pounding at my door.

As I came round, the first thing I noticed was that the light had completely changed. The bright sunny afternoon had gone and it was as black as night outside. I opened the door and asked what was happening. I was told to get into the waiting car immediately because, apparently, a severe tornado warning had just been issued. Only seconds after I jumped into the car, I could see a twister begin to develop right there in the middle of the stadium.

It was an incredible sight to see as it weaved its way around, picking up anything and everything in its path and just sucking it up into the air. At first, it was just chairs and odd items of debris, but soon I could see that the stage itself was being ripped apart. Huge PA cabinets began flying around like leaves in the wind.

My car joined others speeding towards the exit tunnel but just as we entered we encountered a blockage of people on foot who had decided to run there for shelter. The cars inched forward slowly as people began to make their way through but other people coming from behind us were beginning to panic. They started to scrabble over the roof of the car to try and escape. At this point, the roof of the vehicle began to buckle, and the whole situation started to become extremely scary.

Eventually we reached the exit of the tunnel and I will never forget that, just as we cleared the exit, we were hit in the side window by a house brick. The projectile had nothing to do with the twister: someone had thrown it indiscriminately at the car. It is very strange how people sometimes react in times of distress.

I suppose we must have driven for about a minute through a rainstorm, the like of which I have never seen before or since. Each drop of water was almost the size of a golf ball and within less than a minute the water was rising up to the level of the windows of the car. We were forced to stop.

All of a sudden the rain eased, and people were soon swimming around the car and laughing. Almost as fast as it had come, the water subsided and we drove away towards our hotel in Manhattan.

When we arrived back at the hotel, the doorman came out to greet us with a shocked look on his face. 'What on earth happened to you?' he asked.

It was only when we stepped out of the car that we could see why he was so shocked: the car was a complete write-off. In Manhattan, apparently, the weather had been perfect all day.

We returned to play the Roosevelt Stadium show a few days later on 20 August 1974. I remember how eerie it was when Keith opened the show with this noise from his Moog synthesiser that sounded exactly like a howling wind. The whole audience was spellbound in silence as they collectively understood what the sound referred to, and then we segued into 'Hoedown'.

The North American leg of the tour drew to a close on the following night. Although no one realised it at the time, perhaps along with it fell the final curtain upon the golden era of ELP as a band with a shared vision.

We would not perform together again for three years.

CHAPTER 11

A Christmas Intermission

After *Brain Salad Surgery*, Emerson, Lake & Palmer took a break from recording a new studio album. We did try out some material in sessions at Manticore studios, but other things in my life came to the fore, not least the birth of my precious daughter Natasha on 6 March 1975.

It was a life-changing experience being present at the birth. It had a profound effect on my faith in God and gave me an obvious connection to the nativity story. It is a beautiful and enchanting tale which – whether it's true or not – evokes the spirit of Christmas and illuminates the good in humanity.

I had always had a thing about Christmas, in any case. No matter how financially tough it was during my childhood, my parents made sure that it was a time of happiness. I used to love watching my mother cut up the paper chains that would later decorate the sitting room.

We were not a religious family, but my mum and dad were keen to give me the best education they could and arranged for me to attend the regular Sunday school classes at the local church. The strict and intimidating approach there – we were taught to 'Fear the Lord' – was such a contrast from the feeling that I had at home, which was warm, generous and forgiving. Luckily, my parents were not dictatorial or rigid about my religious instruction. I eventually told them that I no longer wanted to attend the Sunday school and they realised that it was unhealthy to force a young child into it. The freedom of choice they gave me then allowed me to revisit the Christian story in my own time later on.

Growing up, I was deeply moved by the famous story about an event that took place in the trenches on the Western Front in 1914, during the First World War. On Christmas Day, the British and German soldiers apparently spontaneously downed their weapons and started singing carols, and played a game of football together in no-man's-land. Even in their darkest and most pitiful hour, it was still possible for a sense of humanity to shine through. Whether you believe in Christianity or not, Christmas is a time of hope, when many of us try to put our troubles to one side and concentrate a little harder on goodwill.

Late in 1974, while Regina was pregnant, Pete Sinfield and I started writing together for what would become *Works Volume 1* at my house in Ascot. I had tuned the bottom string of my guitar from E down to D and started this cascading riff. It was very infectious. I could not get it out of my head. Then it occurred to me – in this half-demented state – that the melody of 'Jingle Bells' fitted over it.

Perhaps this song can be about Christmas too? I thought. So I put the idea to Pete. Neither of us liked the typical party Christmas songs and the serious ones are rare and so hard to write. The more we talked about it, the more we agreed that the reality was that Christmas had become cheapened by commercialism, and that we regretted the loss of childhood innocence. The ideal of 'Peace on Earth and goodwill to all men' had been pushed into the background. This seemed to us reason enough to make a statement. The essence of what we wanted to say was that, despite all the commercialism, it would be good to believe in Father Christmas and the magic of childhood, and to have the joy of giving rather than receiving. Surely – just for one day in the year – this was a spirit worth preserving.

At first, we thought the song would just be an album track. It was recorded at Abbey Road on a hot day in the summer of 1975 with a hundred-piece symphony orchestra and choir assembled and conducted by Godfrey Salmon. A few days before the recording, Godfrey had called me on the phone saying that he felt some trepidation about the possible attitude of the orchestra during this recording session. In those days, classical players were snobbish towards pop and rock musicians and Godfrey wanted to make sure that they started the session in a positive frame of mind.

While on the phone, we racked our brains about how to achieve this but nothing came to mind. So we agreed to give it some thought and talk again later. No sooner had I put down the phone than it rang again and I heard Godfrey's excited voice. He had cracked it! Once the entire orchestra was assembled in the studio and ready to perform, we would dim all the lights and then we would play music from 'The Stripper' over the studio tannoy.

'How is *that* going to help?' I asked him.

Godfrey had a friend who knew a lady who was a profes-sional burlesque feather dancer, and he said that he could probably arrange for her to suddenly appear live in the studio at the appropriate moment. He was convinced that this would break the ice and get the best out of the musicians. Given that I had little previous experience of dealing with orchestras myself, I decided to take his word for it.

The day of the session arrived and the orchestra assembled in the studio. Everyone in the control room had been briefed and knew what was about to happen. The studio lights began to dim and the players looked around wondering what was happening. The music from 'The Stripper' began to play and, through the main studio door, a vivacious Las Vegas showgirl appeared, wearing nothing other than white ostrich feathers. A shockwave passed right through the orchestra.

The showgirl went straight over to the lead violinist and started to bury his face in her huge breasts. He went bright red. He was very straight-laced and really didn't want that sort of attention. Which, of course, amused a lot of the other players. Some of them rushed forward from the back of the orchestra to get a better view. And that's when it started to go wrong.

In the frenzied stampede, one of the trombone players put his foot right through the front of a double bass that had been left lying on the floor. Meanwhile, some of the women in the choir were obviously thinking, '*That's disgusting!*'

The showgirl was only there for five minutes but by the time she left there was total mayhem. This guy crying about his double bass. Angry women. Men cheering. Of course, instead of perking them up, we had to calm them all down.

So, it's true, the recording of our pure and simple Christmas song, 'I Believe in Father Christmas', began with a stripper, lust, anger, tears and destruction. And the whole thing cost me a fortune, not least, as I recall, because I had to pay for the double bass.

Eventually, we tried to convince the orchestra to perform, just to take their minds off it, but of course the studio was still full of chatter and laughter. After allowing everyone finally to settle down and get back to their places, Godfrey raised his baton and we began to record.

The song was captured on the very first pass and that is the version that was used on the original recording. Great players.

And to round off the song, Keith Emerson suggested we use part of the *Lieutenant Kijé* suite by Russian composer Sergei Prokofiev. It worked perfectly.

A couple of months later I received a call from Phil Carson, our label manager at Atlantic Records, telling me that they would like to release 'I Believe in Father Christmas' as a single. I was shocked. I tried to explain that the song was meant to be a serious Emerson, Lake & Palmer album track but he insisted on it. The research they had done had convinced them that it would do well on radio and it was worth giving it a shot. Reluctantly, I agreed to go along with it. It ended up as a solo record released under my own name in November 1975.

To promote the record, we decided to make a video in the archaeological site of Qumran in the Judean Desert in Israel, about an hour-and-half drive from Jerusalem and a few miles from the Dead Sea. Together with Andrew Lane, the ELP tour manager, I flew into Tel Aviv and our music was playing in the terminal as we arrived. This – along with the sight of young civilian teenagers with sub-machine guns strapped to their back – was certainly a first for me.

We stayed at the famous King David Hotel in Jerusalem where there was a reception hosted by the Mayor of Jerusalem, Teddy Kollek, often referred to as 'the greatest builder of Jerusalem since Herod'. He asked if I would one day play in a Roman theatre on the beach at Caesarea, near Tel Aviv.

We then explored the old city of Jerusalem. It was like walking back into the Bible. As I strolled through the covered market, the air was filled with the unmistakable smell of incense and my eyes danced from one sight to the next, never stopping long enough to take it all in. Lamb carcasses hung in the walkway. A young boy passed on a bicycle with live chickens dangling upside down from the handlebars. A priest dressed in black robes and a tall hat rode by on a donkey. Merchants were selling their engraved plates, silk, spices, robes and kaftans and mirrored pillows. It was a scene that probably had not changed much in 2,000 years.

While there, I visited many other famous ancient places such as Bethlehem, the Dome of the Rock, the Mount of Olives and the Western Wall built by King Herod. It felt strange to be a twentieth-century rock musician basically being given a guided tour through biblical history.

Most of the filming took place in the desert. We were accompanied by a small military escort and one of the soldiers explained that the plateau around the Dead Sea gets so hot in the middle of the day that locals refer to it as the Sun's Anvil. To demonstrate, he took a raw egg and cracked it open on the mudguard of his Army truck and it fried almost immediately.

One day, somebody suggested that we should do a special sequence in the caves where the Dead Sea Scrolls were found. It sounded like a good idea until I saw that the caves were situated halfway up a huge cliff face: they were only accessible by helicopter or by inching along a deadly-looking ledge. It was just eighteen inches wide with a sheer drop of hundreds of feet. One false move and it would be all over.

I had been drinking and having a smoke in the limo on the way over, so I took one look at the drop and said, 'No way.'

Before I could add to my protest, I saw the cameraman, with all his gear in hand, moving along the ledge like a tight-rope walker. Having watched him risk his life on my behalf, I had no other choice than to man up and get on with it.

My heart was in my mouth as I inched forward but I reached the other side and felt extraordinarily relieved. Until, that is, the cameraman quietly reminded me that the only way we were going to get back was by doing the same thing in reverse.

We recorded the sequence and, with great care, we all made it back safely.

During my time in Israel, I was given the privilege of sitting among the Bedouins in the desert at sunset. Somebody who had a connection to them had arranged to meet them in the desert at eleven in the morning. We drove out to an oasis with palm trees and a small spring of water. In every direction that I looked, I could see all the way to the horizon. There was nothing but sand dunes.

We waited but there were no Bedouins.

Finally, I asked a security guy where they were.

He said, 'Don't worry, they'll be here shortly.'

'Yeah, but look,' I replied, 'I can see right to the horizon, and there are no Bedouins. How do you think they're going to get all the way from the horizon in the next fifteen minutes?'

'What you don't know is that the Bedouins don't walk over sand dunes,' he explained. 'They walk in between the hills, so you never see them. They're always in the dips of the sand dunes until they get within perhaps 100 yards of you, and then you see them. They never go over a sand dune. It's too much effort, you see.'

Eventually they turned up, almost out of nowhere, just as he said. They were the most beautiful-looking people: pearl-white teeth and teak colouring.

We sat together and were filmed while I played the guitar and they listened. It was an amazing experience. I had the sense of being close to the beginning of civilisation: I was sitting with these ancient people whose story is as old as the sand itself. I didn't know what they were thinking, but they made me feel welcome.

When we returned to the UK and the single was released in November, we were taken aback by the reaction of the public. The song rocketed up the charts. The daily sales figures were astronomical and the only song to outsell it was Queen's 'Bohemian Rhapsody' – it was ironic because I think, in a way, King Crimson and ELP helped opened the door for bands like Queen to draw on European classical music, which they did to great effect. In any other circumstances, I would have been quite peeved to miss out on the number-one slot at Christmas. But with a record like that, which for Queen was also a once-in-a-lifetime recording, I don't think you can complain. I got beaten by one of the greatest records ever made. But I would have been pissed off if I had been beaten by Cliff Richard.

Since then, 'I Believe in Father Christmas' has become a Christmas classic and cover versions have been recorded by numerous artists, from Elaine Paige to U2.

I get a strange feeling when I hear the song playing in department stores at Christmas but when I think about the bigger picture – and its message of peace on Earth and goodwill to all men – I have to say that I'm now quite proud of it. And that means a lot more to me now than the money. That's what people normally want to know. *Greg – what's it like getting those royalty cheques every Christmas?* I wouldn't know. They don't turn up until August.

CHAPTER 12

Fanfare in the Works

*W*orks was too ambitious. To be honest, if it had been left up to me I would not have done it. There were enormous financial risks, which we were warned about repeatedly. In the end it lost us millions of pounds. It was not what ELP fans either wanted or expected from us. There were artistic high points, though, for which I am now grateful, including 'Closer to Believing', 'C'est La Vie' and 'Pirates', which was one of the collective efforts and involved some wonderful music by Keith Emerson.

In the end, it was a simple choice. It came down to either keeping ELP together by incorporating an orchestra or watching the band fall apart. I was still a firm believer in the simple three-piece creative formula, which had delivered such great records and brought so much success for us in the past. Keith, on the other hand, wanted to start work on solo orchestral projects. He was adamant that unless we were prepared to go along with this concept, he did not want to make another Emerson, Lake & Palmer record.

The problem for me was that so many of the qualities that made ELP a great band did not fit into a formal orchestral context: the trademark screaming Hammond organ, for example, or the exciting use of the Moog synthesiser and other pieces of cutting-edge technology, or the use of free-form visionary music on the albums *Tarkus*, *Trilogy* and *Brain Salad Surgery*, or even the use of creative production.

At the time, I think that Keith felt performing with an orchestra would somehow validate him. My view was that the acclaim his work for ELP had received should have been enough. Also, I was concerned that channelling our music through the prism of an orchestra would diminish rather than enhance our power. Everyone other than Keith felt the same way.

However, it seemed such a waste to allow what I felt was a great band to split over the issue. I went against my gut instinct and committed to making the new album a success. In hindsight, this was a critical moment. I should have been stronger and changed direction myself for new pastures green.

Instead, we tried to have it both ways. I cannot remember who came up with the idea, but there was a proposal that we could make a double album which embodied both the solo and the orchestral concepts, and a joint effort from the band. This eventually became *Works Volume 1*: three sides of solo material (one from each of us) and just one side from the three of us working together as a band.

It represented the beginning of the end of Emerson, Lake & Palmer's collective spirit. We had become a group of solo artists collaborating together for the wrong reasons. I no longer felt comfortable producing the records, but I did continue trying to fan a flame that was no longer burning. It was one of my biggest mistakes.

Shortly after the decision about *Works* had been taken in 1976, James Callaghan became Prime Minister. His time in office would see great industrial unrest such as the Winter of Discontent in 1978. The Labour government of the 1970s under Harold Wilson and Callaghan moved to the harder left and pushed forward the belief that wealth should be shared equally. It seemed to me that anyone doing well financially was labelled an enemy of the state.

The Labour solution to the financial crisis was to tax the rich severely. In 1974, they imposed a top rate of tax of 83 per cent on all earned income over £20,000 and 98 per cent on invested income. I'm not saying that people who earn a lot of money shouldn't give back to society, but the mantra at the time seemed to be variants on: *Tax the rich until they squeak.*

Although some rock stars, film actors and writers at the time did undoubtedly earn relatively large sums of money – me included – they were not in the same league as the major property developers and oil tycoons of the day. As a result, there was an exodus of talent from the UK, and many of the people who left were not what you would call 'super-rich'.

None of us in ELP or the road crew wanted to move out of our homes and be forced to live abroad – many of us had young families, and schooling would be disrupted among many other logistical nightmares – but we felt that we had little choice. At the recommendation of our friend Peter Zumsteg, who ran Manticore records and who was a Swiss citizen, we decided to live in Switzerland. Peter told us there was a top recording studio located in Montreux and from there we could easily get back to the UK if need be. We would only be allowed to return to the United Kingdom for a small number of days per year if we did not want to be deemed 'resident' and hit with a huge tax bill.

This instability was deeply emotionally unsettling for some members of the band and crew, and it is clear to me in retrospect how this in turn led to other negative creative, financial and behavioural consequences further down the line. Keith later said that recording in Montreux was the worst mistake we ever made because he thought it made us feel bored and isolated, but it wasn't exactly a hell on earth.

Switzerland is, of course, a beautiful and wealthy place. There are undoubtedly far worse places on earth in which to have to spend a little time. We all lived by the lake in Montreux and it was peaceful and idyllic. The chalet I rented was high up in the mountains overlooking the lake, and I often found myself above the clouds. It was here that Pete Sinfield and I wrote the lyrics to the track 'Pirates', with music by Keith. This was undoubtedly one of the most unusual and vivid of my experiences as a songwriter. There we were, sitting above the clouds in the Swiss alps, writing about sun-drenched Caribbean Islands, pirate ships and buried treasure.

The recording sessions at Mountain Studios in Montreux were a strange affair because we had the studio booked out twenty-four hours a day, seven days a week, so there were no time restrictions on us. We ended up with recording costs of over $1 million.

During one of the final sessions, we spent an afternoon taping with our Swiss orchestra. Thirty seconds from the end of the piece, the orchestra leader suddenly stood up and pointed to his watch. It was time to go. He instructed everyone to put down their instruments. Only thirty seconds left and he was about to ruin an entire afternoon's recording! I was infuriated by how unprofessional and ungracious this was and promptly strode out into the studio and told the musicians that they could now all fuck off and that their services would no longer be required.

The gentleman who owned Mountain Studios was Alex Grobb, who became our friend and helped us in numerous ways during our stay in Switzerland. When he heard about the way the Swiss orchestra had behaved, he was shocked and told us not to worry: he would immediately sort out an alternative. A few hours passed and he came back and told us that he had managed to book a great studio in Paris called Pathé Marconi EMI, and that he could arrange for selected musicians from the Paris Symphony Orchestra to play with us.

One week later, we were sitting in the control room in Pathé Marconi listening to 'Pirates' being performed. It was a joy. Alex then informed us that some of the musicians in the orchestra were due across the road at the Opéra National de Paris to perform a classical concert conducted by Leonard Bernstein. He added that he had known Leonard for a long time and that it might just be possible to get him to come over and take a listen to our new recording of 'Pirates'. We were thrilled at the chance of meeting one of the most famous conductors and composers in the world, and Keith in particular was keen for him to listen to his newly recorded 'Piano Concerto No. 1'. Keith was nervous, though, after all the fuss there had been over his version of Bernstein's 'America' when he was in the Nice.

Alex left the studio and went over to the opera house to meet with Leonard Bernstein while we carried on working. Half an hour later, the studio doors suddenly burst open and Alex returned with the composer and a young friend. Aside from his musical genius, Leonard Bernstein was obviously a colourful character. He wore a red polka-dot neckerchief and was waving a French breadstick around in his right hand. After exchanging greetings, he came and sat down beside me at the recording desk.

'So you've got something to play me then?' he asked.

'Yes,' I replied. 'It's called "Pirates". I hope you like it.'

I pushed the play button and 'Pirates' began to play. Bernstein rested his head on his hands and listened intently as the piece unfolded. When it finished, everyone stood silent waiting for the great man's words. Bernstein slowly turned towards me in his chair and said:

'Singer's not bad.'

He did not seem to realise I was actually the singer. He had probably just assumed that I was the producer. Still, it was one of the best compliments I have ever been paid.

Bernstein made no further comment on the orchestration or the music and so I asked him if he would listen to Keith's 'Piano Concerto No. 1'.

'Sure,' he said.

We played the entire piece through. Again, when it came to an end there was an anxious silence. Bernstein looked thoughtful and then pronounced:

'It reminds me of Grandma Moses.'

Bernstein bade his farewells and disappeared out of the studio to head back to the opera house. We later found out from our record-company president Ahmet Ertegün that Grandma Moses was a renowned American amateur folk artist whose naive paintings suddenly caught the public's imagination when she was in her late seventies.

We returned to Montreux to continue mixing the recordings for *Works*. Despite my concerns that we had lost some of the magic of the original three-piece band, I was starting to feel proud of what we had achieved on the record.

Keith's concerto, on which he was accompanied by the London Philharmonic Orchestra, took up the whole of side one, while my solo side was number two and featured five orchestral numbers, including 'Closer to Believing', 'C'est la Vie' and 'Lend Your Love to Me Tonight', all co-written with Pete. I played acoustic and electric guitar, as well as harmonica on 'Nobody Loves You Like I Do', while 'C'est la Vie' featured a choir and Keith on accordion.

Having my own side on the record at least enabled me to put out in a single go a few of the ballads I had been writing. In normal circumstances, I would only have wanted to put one or a maximum of two ballads on an ELP record because it would have unbalanced the album. Keith was very much about dissonance and I was more of a romantic – even if some of my lyrics were quite dark – and you could say that Carl was somewhere between the two. The reason why ELP worked was because of that dynamic – the contrast of light and shade, power and fragility. Too much of one or the other would have tipped the scales. ELP were still my first priority when it came to music, more than the prospect of going solo – I still thought of us as a family and the balance of the three of us working together was important to me.

Carl Palmer's side had a remake of 'Tank' from our very first album, the funk-rock song 'L.A. Nights', with Joe Walsh from the Eagles on guitar, a big band number called

'Food for Your Soul', and arrangements of pieces by Bach and Prokofiev.

The final side showed that we could still work together as a band, through both 'Pirates' and our arrangement of Aaron Copland's 'Fanfare for the Common Man'.

I enjoyed making 'Fanfare for the Common Man' – I had kept on playing Copland's original when we were working in the studio and Keith and Carl agreed to work on it. The three of us had barely played together in recent times. We were in the studio in Montreux in 1976 and Keith was playing his initial arrangement on his new synthesiser, a Yamaha GX1, when I started to add this shuffle bass line and Carl joined in on the drums – the sound was quite rhythm and blues. The engineer, John Timperley, was recording that first run-through, thank goodness, because that's what is on the record – caught on a single microphone and a two-track tape machine – plus a bit of overdubbing. That piece is the essence of the instrumental side of ELP – it's us in a nutshell.

An edited version of 'Fanfare' became our most successful single ever, reaching number two in the UK charts in July 1977. I wasn't so keen on the edited version because it's like cutting off the corner of a painting – it's not the whole picture – but no one was about to play a nine- or ten-minute track on Radio 1. Aaron Copland's reaction probably brought Keith more happiness than the chart position.

Our manager, Stewart Young, had to get permission from Aaron Copland before we could release it. Copland's publishing company (Boosey & Hawkes again) refused permission and told Stewart that we had no chance of getting it from Copland personally. Stewart persevered and got hold of Copland's home phone number. The composer was upset that the publishing company had not checked with him first, but he told Stewart that it was very unlikely that he would agree to allow us to use 'Fanfare'. Nonetheless, he said he would listen to our version if Stewart sent him a cassette.

The full version was just under ten minutes long and featured a six-minute improvised section. Keith was worried what Copland would think of the improvisation, so he told Stewart to send a three-minute version instead. Stewart then spoke to Copland, who was very friendly, but told him that he could see no reason to allow it, as it was basically just his original theme with a shuffle added. Stewart then told him about the improvised section and sent him the whole piece. In the end, the composer called Stewart back to say, 'This is brilliant, this is fantastic. This is doing something to my music.'

Like Alberto Ginastera when it came to 'Toccata', Copland was willing to go on record praising the piece. Before he died in 1990, he told the BBC (in an interview included on the 2007 ELP compilation *From the Beginning*):

Of course, it's very flattering to have one's music adopted by so popular a group, and so good a group as Emerson, Lake & Palmer ... there was something that attracted me about the version that they perform, which made me think I'd like to allow them to release it. Of course, I always prefer my own version best, but what they do is really around the piece, you might say, rather than a literal transposition of the piece, and they're a gifted group.

The album was released as *Works* on 17 March 1977. By that year everyone was starting to say that 'progressive rock' – whatever that was – was on the decline because of the rise of both disco and punk. We were already having to endure quite a lot of criticism, and because there was, in some people's eyes, a link between progressive rock and pomposity, some journalists were quite personally vitriolic while expressing their glee that our star seemed to be waning. When you are a person in the public eye, you very soon learn to treat the good and bad comments very much the same. I have never thought of myself as a star because – it may be trite to say this but it's absolutely true – we're all the same, we all go to the bathroom and we all have the same problems. So, in a way, by then we had developed an immunity to vicious insults – although I think Keith suffered late in life.

The knives were out but, nonetheless, the album still reached the top ten in the United Kingdom and peaked at number twelve in the United States.

Works soon became known as *Works Volume 1* because we had also written and recorded enough material for another record, *Works Volume 2*, a single album released on 1 November 1977. The album included songs from the *Brain Salad Surgery* era – the song 'Brain Salad Surgery' itself, 'Tiger in a Spotlight' and 'When the Apple Blossoms Bloom in the Windmills of Your Mind I'll Be Your Valentine' – that did not make it on to that album. *Works Volume 2* did not sell as well as *Volume 1* because it was regarded as a compilation of leftover and reissued tracks. Despite this, I'm quite proud of the songs 'Watching Over You', which was a lullaby I wrote for my daughter, 'So Far to Fall' and the ELP versions of 'I Believe in Father Christmas' and 'Show Me the Way to Go Home'. *Works Volume 2* shows some different sides to our music and I don't think it should just be written off.

On our days off in Switzerland, Stewart Young and I would go cycling around Lake Geneva together. We had come across Rochat, a shop that sold immaculate handmade racing bikes which were built as precisely as a Swiss watch. We each bought one and decided to take up cycling.

I have always enjoyed spending time with Stewart. By then he had been managing the band for about four years, and he has continued as my manager for the rest of my career. It was his steady hand on the tiller when ELP went through choppy waters. He is very understanding but allows no room for the sort of silly, impetuous behaviour for which rock musicians are famous. If you have got a friendship that endures for forty years – where you become as close as family – you are very blessed, and until this day we have never had a contract. We have never needed one and we never will. Everything is done on trust.

Starting our rides in Montreux, we would cycle along the smooth tarmac path in the valley basin and ride a few miles around the lake beneath the snow-capped mountains. I will never forget the bright sunshine and cold mountain air, the sound of the gentle ticking of the gears and purring of the tyres as we glided among the birds and butterflies, and the delicate scents of the meadow flowers and sedge grasses. If ever there was an experience of absolute tranquillity on earth, then surely this was it.

With faces red and flushed, we would take a break at a little lakeside restaurant in an enclave called Evian, famous for its bottled mineral water. The restaurant was noted for serving a speciality called *filet de perch*: the freshwater fish, which was caught in the lake, was filleted and fried in butter, then served with French fries and a crisp spring green salad with a French vinaigrette dressing. It was accompanied by the local white wine called Dol and fresh Evian water drawn from the ice-cold waterfall that ran through the grounds of the restaurant. We would invariably finish the meal off with a light dish of wild mountain strawberries called *fraise du bois*, served with homemade vanilla ice cream. In Evian, this meal was simply considered good local grub, but we found it exquisite.

After resting and chatting a while we would set off again on our journey back through the valley, but this time with the afternoon sun on our back. It is hard to describe the feeling you get after a day out riding like this. It is part relaxation, part reinvigoration and part euphoria. Stewart and I still talk about those rides today almost forty years later, and we both marvel at the beauty we witnessed and the lasting impact it had on us.

That's the strange thing about Switzerland. It's almost too beautiful to be true. It was like being a voyeur looking through a window at a magical and surreal fairy-tale landscape.

However, after some time in Switzerland, we got the sense that we were being monitored by the authorities. You rarely if ever see a policeman on the street but you can bet your life that five days before your non-resident visa comes to an end, you will be getting a knock at your door from the man in a long black coat telling you it's time to leave.

During 1977, we decided to relocate to Montreal in Canada for the rehearsals of the *Works* tour. Due to its European heritage, it was a city where we always felt comfortable and received an enthusiastic welcome. We began rehearsals in a dark, vast car park beneath the Montreal Olympic stadium, which had been constructed for the 1976 Summer Olympics.

We soon received a phone call from our UK record company telling us that our recording of 'Fanfare for the Common Man' was climbing fast up the charts. They felt it was going to be a big hit record and asked us to make a video for television. We were deeply involved in rehearsing with the orchestra so our initial reaction was to decline. I said that we couldn't put everything on hold just to make a video. The record

atting with Keith after a sound check. *(© Neil Preston)*

Doing press-ups with David Bowie. We became friendly whilst I was recording *Works Volume 1* in Montreux summer 1976. *(© Kenny Smith)*

When I was recording 'I Believe in Father Christmas', Godfrey Salmon, w assembled and conducted the hundred piece symphony orchestra, arranged fo a professional burlesque feather dance to come to the studio, break the ice ar get the best out of the musicians.
(© Kenny Smith)

uring the filming of the video for 'I Believe in Father Christmas' in the Qumran in the Judean …ert. *(© Kenny Smith)*

…rforming 'C'est La Vie' with ELP. *(© Kenny Smith)*

With American manager Dee Anthony and tour manager Steve Inglis on a private jet. *(© J. Phillip Ra...)*

At the hotel after one of our Madison Square Garden concerts in December 1973.

production rehearsals with ELP's manager, Stewart Young, at the Velodrome in Montreal, early 77, ahead of the tour in May. *(© Kenny Smith)*

ith Keith and Carl in Montreal. *(© Kenny Smith)*

My daughter Natasha, aged three, during the recordings of *Love Beach* at Compass Point studios in the Bahamas. *(© Kenny Smith)*

Playing guitar for California Jam.

ith Ringo Starr and his All-Starr Band in 2001.

ith Roger Daltrey who asked me to play in RD Crusaders and later on The Who track 'Real
ood Looking Boy'.

With my grandson Gabriel in our pirate shirts on his third birthday.

company was disappointed but understood the situation and we left it there.

While this phone call was going on, the orchestra had been stood down for a coffee break. After I hung up, I went upstairs to get some fresh air and a burst of sunlight. I took the elevator up to the ground floor and, as the doors opened, I saw a breathtaking sight. The glorious and futuristic Olympic stadium was covered in a blanket of virgin-white snow, and the Olympic rings were lit up and displayed on huge screens at either end. It was one of those eureka moments. If ever there was a perfect setting for the band to film a video for 'Fanfare for the Common Man', then this had to be it.

The following day, we had a stage erected and the road crew moved our equipment up into the stadium for us to film what would become a classic video. The temperature was below zero and my fingers began to freeze and stick to the steel strings of my bass, so we had to shoot it in bursts of just thirty seconds. It was worth it, though. The record company was thrilled with it and, sure enough, the single went on to become a huge hit.

Once the rehearsals had been completed, we prepared to go on tour with the orchestra. We took 145 people on the road – including our own doctor – and we used a convoy of eleven tractor-trailers and four tour buses. I was informed that one of the trucks was dedicated solely to the carrying of spares. It was a gargantuan operation – it was like a travelling city. We had to book up entire hotels.

I was looking for the tour manager Tommy Mohler one day and I went from floor to floor of a hotel yelling: 'Is Tommy here?' I noticed in each corridor that there were buckets and buckets with upturned wine bottles in them, and I suddenly realised we were paying for all that. It was an awakening, but huge costs seemed to be part and parcel of ELP.

'It's like this,' I said to an interviewer at the time. 'Everyone criticises ELP. They say the band has too much fuckin' money. What we do is reinvest it back into ourselves as entertainment. Anyone who had anything to do with the financing of this project thought we were crazy. Our heads are on the *block*. It's not the first time and probably won't be the last. I'm glad. It's not just a question of another rock show hitting Pittsburgh. It's a question of presenting a *show* again, one *magic* night.' I thought we had a responsibility to deliver the best possible entertainment, every single night.

There was a wonderful sense of camaraderie and excitement as the tour kicked off. The young musicians who made up the orchestra were the top classical players emerging from the best music academies in the United States, and each one was dedicated to making this show as good as it could possibly be. We could all feel that we were a part of something unique. This bond became profound as the tour went on.

For me, the orchestral tour was a challenging departure from performing as a three-piece band. Instead of locking up with Keith and Carl as before and playing instinctively off each other, we were now under the control of a conductor.

We would often find ourselves having to adjust the tempo in order to stay within the feel being set by the orchestra.

Also, the audience reaction was different now. Perhaps the sense of formality that inhabits – and inhibits – standard orchestral shows made the audience reserved or maybe, like me, they sensed that something had changed because the band itself was not in full control of the music.

We did achieve some spectacular moments, such as the performance at the Olympic Stadium in Montreal and the shows we played at Madison Square Garden, but the response was sometimes held back compared to the raw excitement we were able to generate on our own. We were not just playing orchestral pieces from *Works*, but giving the full treatment to pieces from throughout our career, including 'Tarkus' and 'Pictures from an Exhibition'.

On Sunday 12 June 1977, we were performing at the Veterans Memorial Auditorium in Des Moines, Iowa. I was standing backstage waiting to do the sound check when Stewart came over to me and whispered into my ear that he needed to speak to me urgently. We found a quiet place away from all the noise and hustle and bustle, and sat down together. I could see by the look on his face that something was wrong.

There was a brief moment of silence before he looked me in the eyes and said: 'We have to stop this tour.'

He explained that the tour expenses were costing over $300,000 a week. The concerts were selling out, but we were going to lose millions. Just one or two cancellations had thrown the whole finances off-kilter.

Stewart informed Keith and Carl and, after a brief discussion, we decided to be honest straight away with the orchestra and everyone else involved in the tour. We told them we would only be able to hire the orchestra for a few individual dates at large venues later in the tour. The atmosphere was sombre as the news spread. We all felt a deep sense of loss. Despite my misgivings about using an orchestra, we had become something of a family again.

A little while after the announcement, a few of the musicians came to Stewart's room with tears in their eyes. They told him that the orchestra had held a meeting and that they had been having such a great time on the tour that they had all agreed to continue playing without any fees: they just wanted food and lodging. Unfortunately, we couldn't do that as the musicians' union, the American Federation of Musicians, would not allow it.

We continued as a trio and the orchestra did not return until we went to New York for a three-night stint at Madison Square Garden, starting on 7 July 1977. Keith once said: 'The second night at Madison Square Garden was the best gig of the whole tour for me. I finished playing my piano concerto with this splendid orchestra, and I received a standing ovation that must have lasted three minutes. Greg bounced on the stage and hugged me in front of 14,000 people. After all the hard work and arguing he hugged me! That meant a lot.'

On 26 August, we played with the orchestra for the final time. We were back at the Olympic Stadium in Montreal and there was so much pressure on us. There was only time for one orchestral rehearsal, and we had not played together for a while so everybody was rusty. We also had serious technical difficulties trying to incorporate the first ever digital multi-track tape machine into the live PA mixing desk. In the end, we had to record the whole show on a two-track stereo machine but we were still able to capture a great recording of the band with the orchestra we had assembled for the *Works* tour.

The Montreal show was sold out, with over 80,000 fans helping to bring the band and its performance to a whole new level of excitement. Having that wall of beautiful sound behind us again made for an intense evening of music. We incorporated rock treatments, unplugged acoustic numbers and traditional classical arrangements – so in a way it encapsulated our career together. For many in the audience, it was overwhelming. Fans have told me they cried during some of the more tender moments in the show; and songs like 'Knife-Edge' from the *Emerson, Lake & Palmer* debut album were more powerful than ever before because of the orchestra.

Whenever I am in Canada, I run into people who were there and they always say it was the most magnificent live concert they have ever attended. For me, it remains one of the most memorable shows of my entire career.

For the second half of the *Works* tour, from late 1977 and into March 1978, we toured as a three-piece for financial reasons and argued quite a lot. I don't think any of us really enjoyed it, even though the fans did. Something was missing.

One side effect of going on tour with the orchestra was that it meant that I would have another chance to see the King of Rock and Roll, though sadly this was very much towards the end of his life.

A short while ago I received a letter from Danny Markus, an old friend who lived in New York and worked for Atlantic Records, which included his reminiscing about the time our paths crossed with Elvis – and the letter also gives a large clue as to why our orchestral tour lost so much money. In 1976, in the year before the tour, Stewart Young was staying in Danny's second bedroom, as many Atlantic managers did, while he was in New York.

One night the phone rings in my apartment. The voice at the other end says, 'This is Colonel Tom Parker,' in a relaxed gravely southern voice. 'May I please speak to Stewart Young?' The Colonel dials his own calls. I made a note. Every second, when you are on with him, is a learning moment. He is the manager of all managers. He was the master of perception being everything.

So this was business and the Colonel was on the line. I brought the phone over to Stewart. He is a tall, good-looking man with financial skills and tough negotiating positions but he isn't much of a talker. It sounded like Elvis's manager was dealing the cards. Stewart hung up and briefed me on his call. Seems Elvis will be on tour next summer [1977] and they need the Louisville Fairgrounds on one of the nights ELP had booked it for their orchestra tour.

I had seen drawings and Polaroids of the ELP set. They were planning to take a seventy-piece orchestra from city to city. The usual way to do this would be to pick up musicians in each town and rehearse them at sound check for that evening's performance, which saved a lot of money in transportation and hotel rooms. Sinatra worked this way. He just brought a rhythm section and his band leader.

ELP saw it differently. It would be baseball stadiums for the most part and there would be complex sound issues and logistics. When the road manager walked up to the hotel front desk there would be 125 rooms under his name. Buses with drivers for the orchestra, trucks with drivers with the staging, ELP with an airplane. *This is going to blow the audience away*, I thought. No one had ever toured America like this. Maybe one or two dates or a sit down. Not forty-five cities. Few would take this financial risk even in those days. ELP did and it was costly. But what price art?

The date the Colonel was interested in was smack in the middle of this tour. It was a routing issue as Louisville fit right into Elvis's schedule. The Colonel asked what he should give in return for having ELP's intricate set pulled back on the stage for one night. Not torn down. Just pulled back if possible and covered.

'Elvis doesn't need the set,' said the Colonel. 'He is the set.'

The Colonel would pay expenses. But what else?

We tossed ideas back and forth but really in a situation like this, manager to manager, all that was necessary, Stewart said, was a row of seats and a guaranteed audience with the King.

And what British band, any band for that matter, would turn down meeting Elvis Presley? ELP would love that and most likely they will need some entertainment themselves in the middle of putting their tour together.

The following July it all came together. The Best Western in Louisville was not the best hotel in town but it was right across the way from the Fairgrounds. And Elvis was staying there. We saw him go through the lobby out to a car on the day of his show. We saw the scrum that surrounded him as he moved about in public. It was one of the Colonel's tricks to build mystique which he had learned during his carnival days.

Even though I could hit a golf ball and strike the venue from the hotel, we took three limousines to the show. We had our own row near the front. As soon as we sat down the house lights dimmed and the Elvis Presley Band started a medley of the King's hits. Then Elvis came out and our row gasped. He was bloated. I couldn't make out a word he was singing. It was like Dean Martin playing the drunk. He forgot some lyrics on the second song. On the third song he came to the front of the stage, stuck out his belly, patted it on the top and made some crack about a baby. I covered my face because I feared that the buttons and other hardware were going to come flying off that white jumpsuit he was wearing.

After the fourth song started we all looked at each other down the row. Without saying a word we stood up simultaneously – Keith, Greg, Carl, Stewart, their road manager, bodyguards, and their Atlantic representative – and headed back to our waiting cars and the hotel. We walked out on the King that night and, though I have seen ELP over the years, separately and together, we have never discussed that show.

As I read Danny's account, I could vividly recall that sad feeling as I watched Elvis in such bad shape, struggling to perform on our stage. The strangest thing was that the audience behaved as though nothing was wrong and that it was simply the Elvis they had always known and loved. That was probably the most tragic aspect of it.

A month after this show, on 16 August 1977, I was in Las

Vegas, sitting in the back of a car outside my hotel. As usual in Vegas, the hotels were so busy you had to wait before unloading your bags. Suddenly, the driver turned around to me.

'You'll never believe what I've just heard come over the intercom,' he said. 'Elvis is dead.'

Just as the initial shock subsided I looked out and saw the lights along the strip getting switched off. Las Vegas without the lights is an eerie and depressing place indeed. People came pouring out of the casinos, looking shaken, many in tears. It was as though there had been an earthquake or some other kind of catastrophe. All the casinos were closed down that night as a mark of respect. It felt at that moment like Las Vegas would be changed forever.

The United States had always been a place of great joy, optimism and possibilities for me, and part of that stemmed from the second Emerson, Lake & Palmer tour and seeing Elvis in his charismatic prime at Lake Tahoe in 1971.

Eight years later, I had witnessed the King's fall from grace, while my own band ELP was in both a creative and a financial mess. It felt like the end of an era.

CHAPTER 13

Outro: Loveless Beach

I believe that the orchestral project ultimately led to the demise of ELP. Prior to the orchestra and *Works Volume 1*, ELP were a multiple-platinum-album-selling act, performing in stadiums and arenas all over the world, inspiring a whole new generation of musicians. After the orchestral project, we were supposed to pare back our stage show and the innovative recordings dried up. To me, it seemed that the flame of ELP that had ignited so many audiences throughout the world had begun to die.

Following on from the orchestral projects, all three of us felt in need of a break from each other and a time away from the pressures of being in ELP. We had a meeting in New York with the president of Atlantic Records, Ahmet Ertegün, and explained to him our collective decision to take a time away from the Emerson, Lake & Palmer circus. In the meantime, each of us would make a solo album.

It was immediately apparent that Ahmet was not pleased with this plan. He told us in no uncertain terms that under the terms of our contract, we still owed Atlantic one more album and that if we did not deliver this we could be assured that none of our solo projects would ever enjoy the type of support that we had been used to getting in ELP.

This was delivered as a fait accompli.

In spite of the fact that as artists we really did not want to embark on a new album project, we were faced with no other option than to press on and deliver this one last recording.

It just so happened that by that particular time all three of us had established homes in Nassau in the Bahamas, and I also knew that my old friend Chris Blackwell, the president of Island Records, had recently built a recording studio there called Compass Point. It was located on a stretch of the island called Love Beach, which is how we came by the title of the album. We didn't like the title. The fans didn't like the title. In fact, no one liked the title except Atlantic. Keith said that he phoned Ahmet Ertegün to try and change it, but was told that titles didn't matter anyway and Atlantic were going to stick with it.

The cover was a departure too, with a photograph of us smiling with bright-white teeth, chest hair on show and a background of a palm tree and clear skies. It was a shock to most of the fans after the likes of the H. R. Giger cover for *Brain Salad Surgery*. The cover said commercial MOR, not ELP. We looked like the Bee Gees on holiday.

It felt like Atlantic were trying to force ELP into a commercial gap that their marketing men thought existed, irrelevant of the band or the music. It was an obvious case of trying to force a square peg into a round hole.

It was clear from the beginning that none of us would have really chosen to make this record, but once we had been forced to do it, we all undertook to put our shoulders to the wheel – at least when it came to making the music – and make it as good as we could.

Under the given circumstances, I did not feel at the time that it would be honest or appropriate for me to produce this album so I decided to devote my efforts entirely to the writing and performing. My old friend Pete Sinfield came to the island for a while and we wrote some of the material together – the title track, 'All I Want Is You', 'Taste of My Love' and 'For You'. Pete, Keith and I wrote 'The Gambler', and we drew 'Canario' from Spanish composer Joaquín Rodrigo's *Fantasía para un gentilhombre*, which was written in the 1950s. As was traditional for an Emerson, Lake & Palmer album, we included a long, multi-part piece, 'Memoirs of an Officer and a Gentleman', but unusually Carl and I did not have a hand in writing it. Keith worked on the twenty-minute, four-part piece with Pete. By then, the fact was that Pete and I were coming to the end of our writing partnership.

Keith ended up doing most of the producing and mixing of the tracks, which he was not too happy about. Carl and I left Nassau as soon as we could.

Even though there are a couple of nice things on the *Love Beach* record, for me at least it is not one of the great highlights of the band's recording career. However, when I come to think about the circumstances surrounding how it got made, then I hope that we did still at least manage to maintain the long-standing reputation ELP had for making good-quality records.

The album, our seventh studio recording, was released in the United Kingdom on 18 November 1978. We performed 'All I Want Is You' on *Top of the Pops* but otherwise we didn't really promote the album or support it with a tour. Unsurprisingly, it initially did not do too well on either side of the Atlantic, although it eventually sold enough records to go gold in the United States and silver in the United Kingdom, and its merits have undergone something of a reappraisal in more recent times.

Once the album had been completed, we all went our own separate ways, each of us working on our own individual projects. The band split without even doing a farewell performance.

Emerson, Lake & Palmer, at least for the time being, were no more.

Part Three

CHAPTER 14

Life after ELP

After we had completed the *Love Beach* album, I set off for Los Angeles to begin a new chapter in my career. Rushing headlong into this was probably a mistake. What I should have done was taken a break away from music altogether for a while, if only to regain my equilibrium and recharge my batteries.

I had a sense of liberation, but also a sense of loss. I think that anyone who has lived through the experience of being part of a stadium-level rock band will immediately identify with what happens to you when that band comes to an end. For so many years, the band has become your entire life. Both your musical identity and indeed your entire personality have been totally dedicated to the band and, when the band is no more, you inevitably feel confused and disorientated. It really does take some considerable time to stop thinking in terms of the band and start rediscovering your own musical identity, and perhaps even your personal identity as well. I can see now that starting to work in LA so quickly after finishing *Love Beach* denied me the time and space I required to make the necessary adjustment.

When I initially began songwriting in LA, my mind would almost always wander and I would find myself envisaging the finished record with keyboards playing a central part in the overall production. I suppose that I still instinctively imagined Keith Emerson playing a role in shaping the song and the sound. I wasn't thinking like 'Greg Lake'; I was still thinking like 'Lake' from Emerson, Lake & Palmer.

Of course, the fact was that I was no longer restricted to the keyboard-based structure of ELP, and I was free to follow any musical path I chose. This was probably a bit of a mixed blessing. On the one hand, I now had complete freedom of choice, musically, but on the other, this presented the danger of opening up far too many doors simultaneously, which could then possibly result in the album having no coherent or unified direction.

In the end, I discovered that the answer to this dilemma, and therefore the key to my own musical identity, lay in the reason I began to play music in the first place: the magic of the guitar. I had played some guitar when I was with ELP, but it was rarely the focus of the writing and I had often played bass instead because it suited the collective sound. When the band dissolved, I started to discover the true magic of the instrument – and its importance to me – again.

From that point forward, I was no longer bound to use synthesisers or have obligatory keyboard solos, and would now be able to return to a more eclectic way of writing and recording, rather in the same way as the first King Crimson album had been made. But this time, I would usually have a guitar, not a bass, in my hands.

Shortly after arriving in Los Angeles, I rented a house in Benedict Canyon and it was there that I first met up with the American songwriter Steve Dorff. Steve had recently co-written 'I Just Fall in Love Again' for an album by the Carpenters, which became a hit for Anne Murray in 1979. He has written dozens of country hits, and has become well known for composing film and television themes – he's been nominated for a hatful of Grammy and Emmy awards.

I began to work with him on a song that he had co-written called 'Let Me Love You Once Before You Go', which he wanted me to record. We would often work up at the house preparing the arrangement and discussing how we would set about recording the song and so on. In the end, W. G. Snuffy Walden from Stray Dog, who had been signed to ELP's Manticore label, did the guitar solo on 'Let Me Love You Once Before I Go'. Snuffy went on to win an Emmy for writing the music for *The West Wing*.

Shortly before Steve Dorff and I collaborated, Steve had been working on the soundtrack he had written for the Clint Eastwood film, *Every Which Way but Loose*, using Toto to perform most of the backing tracks. He felt that they would also be the perfect musicians for me to work with on the new record. My friend and co-manager at the time, Alex Grobb, whom I had got to know in Montreux, also knew the band well and so we set up a date to record Steve's song along with two other songs that I had written.

Being in a band like ELP, you play more or less the same ten or twenty songs with the same couple of people for ten or twenty years, and you don't get much exposure to other musicians, other forms of music and other ways of doing things. It's a wonderful thing when a current of fresh air blows and you feel a wholly different influence, another style.

During the Toto sessions, I was stunned by their musicianship and how incredibly fast they worked; each member of the band was a master in his own right. I will never forget watching the late and great Jeff Porcaro on drums – everything he played just seemed effortless and his 'feel' is undoubtedly among the best you will ever hear. (Just take a listen, for example, to 'Rosanna' or 'Africa' by Toto to hear the master of feel at work.) One of the things that I immediately noticed about Jeff's playing was just how little he used his cymbals. When I asked him why this was, he told me that, in doing so many recording sessions in Los Angeles, he had discovered that the overall production sounded much clearer and cleaner without the constant hiss of cymbals going on throughout the recording. He was absolutely right because the fact is that cymbals occupy a very similar frequency to certain elements of the human voice and this conflict causes all sorts of problems when it comes to balancing and perspective in the final mix.

Steve Lukather was another wonder to behold. Watching his fingers glide effortlessly across the fretboard was, and still is, an unforgettable experience. David Paich, the keyboard player, songwriter and producer, is simply a genius. Last but definitely not least, the legendary David Hungate on bass is also outstanding. All in all, Toto are about as good as it gets when it comes to musicianship.

I spent another couple of months writing in LA and living the Californian dream. This was all well and good, I suppose, but LA exists in its own bubble and after a while I began to feel rather cut off from the rest of the world. I think that perhaps this might have had something to do with the fact that the time difference between the West Coast and the United Kingdom is so drastic, and also that, being a European, I began to suffer from some sort of cultural deficiency.

In any case, I decided to return to England to live a more rural life in Dorset, where I had recently bought a mill house along with a beautiful stretch of the River Allen.

Having enjoyed my recent experience with Toto, I was reminded of just how important it was for me to have my own band, and so this was another motivating factor for me to return to the UK.

As soon as I arrived back home, I immediately started work on building a recording studio at the mill. I soon realised that was going to take some considerable time to complete so, while the work was ongoing, I continued recording at Abbey Road in London in 1980–81.

For my debut solo record, I wanted to pay tribute to Bob Dylan by recording one of his songs. I had always been a huge fan of Bob and his songwriting, and I felt that this was as good a time as any for me to pay my respects. The only thing was that I did not really want to do one of his big hits, but rather something less well known. Just purely by coincidence, Tommy Mohler, one of my tour managers at the time, used to work for Bob. He asked him if he had any unreleased material that I could record. Bob explained that he didn't have any completed songs, but that he did have one song that was halfway written and that he would be more than happy for me to complete it. The title of the song was 'Love You Too Much'. As a result, I share a co-writing credit with the legendary Bob Dylan (plus Helena Springs). Having finished the writing, I began to record the track at Abbey Road.

By the time we came close to finishing the recording, my instincts told me that there was something about the overall production that was missing. What I could hear going on in my mind was a blistering rock guitar part that would lift the excitement level of the track so high that it would help under-pin the title, in the sense of almost being 'too much'.

On a good day, I am not too bad a guitar player myself, but what I could hear in my mind was a guitar part that I knew would be something far beyond my own capability, so

I asked my managers if they knew anyone who could possibly fit the bill.

Within an hour, I got a phone call back from Stewart Young, saying that he thought that Gary Moore would be a good choice. Of course, I knew of Gary's previous work with Thin Lizzy, and he had just had a big solo hit with 'Parisienne Walkways'. He had a reputation for being a great player – one of the very best – so I asked Stewart to see if Gary would like to play on the record.

The next day we were back in the studio and Gary had been booked to play the session. I will always remember him walking into the control room in Abbey Road in a long black leather coat, carrying his guitar case and looking just a little shy.

As soon as we had exchanged greetings, Gary plugged in his guitar and, without even taking off his coat, he immediately put on his headphones and started to play.

I asked him if he would like to come into the control room and take a listen to the track but he said that he would rather just play along in real time. Luckily we had the good sense to record the first take; as is so often the case, it was a good thing that we did as this is the actual guitar part you hear on the record today. Gary's track was done in one single pass having never heard the song before.

To be honest, we were all absolutely floored by his performance and, when the track finished, everybody in the control room instantly stood up and applauded.

I knew right then that I had found the right guitarist for my band.

During my career, I have always considered myself to be very fortunate to have worked with some of world's greatest musicians and the band that I formed during the Abbey Road sessions was no exception.

Apart from Gary, we had the one and only Tommy Eyre on keyboards. Tommy is probably best known for his work with Joe Cocker and the Grease Band – he played the Hammond organ on Joe's version of the Beatles classic 'With a Little Help from My Friends'. He also played with Gerry Rafferty on 'Baker Street' and recorded an album with the legendary guitarist John Martyn. Strangely enough, shortly after working with me, he became the musical director of Wham! and apparently had a hand in hits like 'Wake Me Up Before You Go-Go', 'Freedom' and George Michael's 'Careless Whisper'. Tommy was a truly wonderful musician and an amazing character. Just like Joe Cocker, he grew up in Sheffield and radiated that same warm, 'salt of the earth' personality that people from that part of the world are so famous for.

On bass, we had Tristram Margetts. I had known Triss for many years from back in my old home town of Poole in Dorset, and he and his brother had been members of Spontaneous Combustion, whose debut album I had helped to produce in the early 1970s.

The drummer was Ted McKenna who for many years had

played with the Sensational Alex Harvey Band, with whom Tommy had also played for a while. Ted was a terrific player with a great instinctive feel. My old bandmate Michael Giles from King Crimson days also helped out on drums.

Apart from the core band and Toto, we also had the good fortune to have Clarence Clemons from Bruce Springsteen's E Street Band come in to play the sax solo on the song 'Someone'. Every time I hear him play that solo, even to this day, it still makes the hair on the back on my neck stand up.

One of the wonderful things about playing with such great musicians happens when it comes to leaving the studio and performing live. When I made the *Greg Lake* solo album and heard some of the breathtaking performances that occurred during the recording, I simply had no concept of what could possibly be done to improve upon them. However, the answer soon became apparent when we started to perform these songs live, starting at the Reading Festival at the end of August 1981. It was then that I came to realise that the performances on the record were simply one facet of what these magnificent players were capable of achieving.

Night after night, I would hear Gary play his solos in a slightly different way and always better than he had done on the previous night, and Tommy would instantly respond with a seemingly endless stream of musical imagination in the form of responsive chord inversions along with wonderful melodic inventions. For me, there is almost no better feeling on earth than to play music with a band of great musicians.

We recorded Gary Moore's 'Nuclear Attack' for the album, and apart from the Steve Dorff song and the Dylan track, I wrote the other songs such as 'It Hurts' and 'For Those Who Dare' either by myself or with Tony Benyon, with Tommy contributing to a couple of tracks. When I listen back to these recordings, both in the studio and live, all I can say is that I am extremely proud of them and eternally grateful to all the musicians who helped to make them what they are. I should also express my deep gratitude to all of the recording engineers and other contributors who worked so hard on the record and made it all come together.

The album, simply entitled *Greg Lake* and produced by me, was released by Chrysalis records on 25 September 1981. In terms of sales, at least when compared to the early days of Emerson, Lake & Palmer, it did not do that well. However, with the benefit of hindsight, I think that if any solo artist today had similar initial sales figures, the champagne corks would immediately start popping. I think that Chrysalis simply expected to cash in on ELP's success and carry on as if nothing had happened. Unfortunately, this was a rather naive assumption because, as far as the record-buying public are concerned, a band is one entity and a solo artist who may have come from that band is quite another.

I persevered, despite feeling that Chrysalis were not really interested in working hard with me to make sure the music was heard and promoted in the right way. My second solo album, called *Manoeuvres*, was released in July 1983. All the band members, including Gary Moore, had faith in what I was doing and were happy to reunite to work on the album.

I wrote the title track with Gary, and we also wrote 'I Don't Want to Lose Your Love Tonight' together and recorded his song 'A Woman Like You'. Triss Margetts and Tony Benyon worked with me on 'Haunted', and we recorded 'Famous Last Words' written by Chris Bradford, Andy Scott and David Most. I wrote the rest of the album, and like the first one, produced it. It was not as heavy or guitar-driven as the first solo album – it has a more melodious feel, and I think some of those songs have stood the test of time. It didn't sell well – there was no tour and virtually no promotion – although like the first album I have noticed in later years that some writers have reappraised it very positively.

I went up to Chrysalis's office one day to meet the president, Chris Wright, and listened to him express his disappointment at my sales figures. He then asked me if I could possibly write another 'Lucky Man'? I knew in that single moment that my relationship with Chrysalis was definitely not destined to endure.

Of course, no artist likes to feel that they have come short of expectations or disappointed anyone, and at that time I had no perception of what was or was not a realistic expectation in terms of sales. Now, I think that if Chrysalis had been more committed and had been prepared to work hard for the success they wanted to achieve, then the future could have been different. However, in the music business, the same as it is in life, one simply has to accept the good along with the bad and move on. I do not harbour any regrets or resentment.

I always had time for new acts and younger people kicking the arses of bands like ELP that dominated the music season in the early and mid-1970s. When I was a young boy, I can remember begging my dad to stop playing his Bing Crosby records. If young people didn't come forward and try to get rid of the older geezers, then there would be no fun in music and, creatively, it would die. I was not a fan of everything that happened in the punk era, but I liked the Sex Pistols and *Never Mind the Bollocks*. There was a point to it.

I felt disconnected from the musical culture of the 1980s, though. It seemed to me that the real essence of rock and roll had been lost. Still today, there is little sense of true creative musical identity in the work of many artists – when you listened to Jimi Hendrix, Pink Floyd and hopefully ELP, you knew who it was immediately because they were naturally distinct and innovative. In the 1980s, creativity and passion seemed to be replaced by product. Fashions and genres, maybe starting with the New Romantic movement, were now more important than the music itself. There were too many trends that ended up being a bit ephemeral – here today and gone tomorrow. Too many artists of my generation were releasing gratuitous solo albums, borrowing from the new trends, just to try to remain relevant.

My own solo records went in the wrong direction, too. I had played with keyboards throughout the 1970s, but I'm a guitar player and so I desperately wanted an opportunity to play with other guitar players. But, as far as the record business and the record-buying public were concerned, that direction wasn't the best thing for my career – purely in terms of popularity, it was a real mistake.

After those two solo albums, I had no appetite or inspiration for creating popular music in what I saw as an increasingly phony, media-driven world. My philosophy at the time, as indeed it still is today, is that if you have nothing worthwhile to say then it is better to remain silent. I was happy in Dorset with my family, fishing and tending to the land and the river.

I had also come to accept that nothing I could do in the future was ever likely to match up to the worldwide success and recognition Emerson, Lake & Palmer and King Crimson had achieved. It was not realistic to expect to find the same level of success with a third group or as a solo artist – hardly anyone in the history of music has achieved that. I still loved music and playing the guitar but now I did this purely for pleasure. It felt so different from performing as a professional musician. I didn't have to be competitive or try to meet a challenge.

This reclusive period of my music career didn't last long, however.

■ ■ ■

In late 1983, I received a call from Carl Palmer. He asked if I could do him a small favour. I thought he wanted to borrow a guitar or something so I immediately said: 'Sure. What is it?'

He told me that Asia had encountered a problem.

Carl had co-founded Asia in 1981 with John Wetton, who was in King Crimson after I had left, and two members of Yes – the guitarist Steve Howe and the keyboardist Geoff Downes. For those that like the labels 'progressive' and 'supergroup', the formation of Asia was a dream come true. While progressive rock was supposed to have died with the advent of punk, new wave, disco, New Romanticism and all the other genres, Asia had bucked the trend and their debut album was top of the US album chart for nine weeks in 1982, but their sound was more like commercial rock music.

When Carl phoned me, Asia were under contract to play a huge MTV and Westwood One Radio Network simulcast of the band's sold-out show at Tokyo's Nippon Budokan arena. MTV had even chartered a Boeing 747 jet to transport a number of prizewinners to see the show.

But there had been a problem with their singer and bass player John Wetton. Would I be prepared to step in and take John's place for that event and the rest of the Japan tour?

John and I grew up close to each other on the south coast of England and were good friends. It felt disloyal to step into his band. However, Carl explained that he had spoken to John and he was happy for me to take over his role for these shows.

I then asked Carl when these shows were scheduled to take place. There was a brief silence.

'Well,' Carl eventually muttered sheepishly, 'they're due to start in two weeks.'

'Please tell me you're not serious!' I replied. 'How can I learn the entire Asia catalogue and then perform it live on satellite by then? I'd love to help but I just can't see a way to make it happen.'

A few hours passed by and then the phone calls began to come in from Asia's label, Geffen Records. John Kalodner, Brian Lane and finally David Geffen himself pleaded with me to at least give it a try. They were so financially committed to this project that there would be serious repercussions if it collapsed.

In the end – and against my own better judgement – I agreed to help Carl out. He was my close friend, after all. And Geffen offered me so much money there was no way I could refuse it.

Over the next two weeks, I worked day and night to get the material under control. John Wetton and Geoff Downes are excellent songwriters, and the songs had catchy hooks, so the learning process was smoother than I had expected it to be. But to learn someone's entire set and all the nuances, all the cues and all the little points, to remember all the chord shifts and make the lyrics sound the same as the record – it was a huge undertaking. I would not want to do it again.

When it came to the show, I had a lyric prompter but I got through it. Miraculously, the satellite broadcast on 6 December 1983 went off without a hitch.

My time spent with Asia, however, was not enjoyable. To me, a band should have an underlying bond rather like a family, and I think that in Asia's case, Geffen's A & R man John Kalodner had more or less brought the band together in the first place. I have never been one of those artists who flit between bands like jumping on and off a roundabout. I always liked Carl, but Asia were a funny bunch at that time. Everyone was trying to fire everyone else. There were huge conspiracies. You would walk down the corridor and there would be people plotting to fire each other in every room you walked into. It was hilarious.

Also, I simply did not want to go in that corporate rock direction. I could see that would be a fast way to finish me off in creative terms. So after the Japan concerts, I said, 'If this band's going to have me in it, it would at least need to have some authentic musical foundation.'

And that was where we parted company.

In 1985, Keith Emerson and I were offered a recording contract by an old friend, Jim Lewis from Polygram Records. The proposal was that we re-form Emerson, Lake & Palmer to make another album, but Carl Palmer was still involved with Asia and wasn't available.

Keith and I were not initially inspired by the idea from an artistic standpoint, but we had nothing better to do at the time and there was a substantial sum of money on the table. Jim Lewis reassured us that we could go ahead without Carl, given that Keith and I wrote most of the material in ELP. We did indeed also have a backlog of songs we had written since the band had broken up.

So we decided to audition various drummers and almost hired a very good one called Tony Beard, who went on to play for Mike Oldfield and all sorts of other artists. But word about what we were up to had already begun to spread around the industry and one morning we received a phone call from Cozy Powell.

We had known Cozy for many years through his work with Jeff Beck, Rainbow and Whitesnake – and he and Keith both loved motorcycles. We agreed to meet up with him at Keith's house in Sussex for a jam.

Cozy's style was different from that of Carl Palmer. He was a heavy metal drummer, far more solid and earthy than Carl, whose playing tends to be fast, light and technical. Keith and I were both impressed by the power and simplicity Cozy brought to existing ELP material such as 'Tarkus', 'Fanfare for the Common Man' and 'Karn Evil 9'. The three of us were excited about the possibilities for this new era of the band.

The press immediately fell on the fact that Cozy's last name began with a 'P' and were convinced that this was the reason he was chosen. This was certainly not the case. He could have been Cozy Smith or Cozy Jones: we would still have hired him. It was just a fortuitous coincidence. We were a bit embarrassed about it, actually. (As Cozy said in an interview in *Creem* in 1986: 'Porcaro, Phillips, Peart, Ian Paice is another one . . . there's a lot of drummers whose names start with P.' Keith once joked that we also checked out Ringo Parr.) The truth was that Cozy simply fitted the bill.

It was a pleasure to work with him, and he enjoyed it too. People like to think that Keith and I were perpetually at war with each other, which wasn't true. Cozy would be asked the leading question of what it was like to work with us, but he said it was the most pleasurable working relationship he had ever had.

I was pleased to be working with Keith again. The end of the original ELP was not one of those band break-ups where there is a lot of recrimination, bitterness and mudslinging. The three of us just felt simultaneously that we had been pushed too hard and too far, especially through the touring, and we did not want to keep on going out and flogging ourselves, purely for commercial reasons. Since the band had split up, while I was doing my solo albums and Carl was in Asia, Keith had done a reggae-influenced album in the Bahamas and composed the film soundtracks to *Inferno* and *Nighthawks*.

The veteran engineer Tony Taverner and I co-produced the recordings, which were made in 1985 and 1986, and all the songs involved Keith and I working together on the writing or arranging. We lost some of the material when Keith's studio, in a converted barn, was destroyed in an accident involving an out-of-control tractor carrying some logs, and we had to move to another studio.

We resisted the temptation to follow the fashionable adult-oriented rock style, which had been so successful for Asia and Yes, who had re-formed in 1983 and had their biggest-selling album ever. We did not want to sound exactly like we did back in the 1970s – we were Emerson, Lake & Powell now, not ELP – but we wanted to stay true to our ethos of pushing boundaries and exploring new sounds. The further we went along, we realised that the latest technology in the hands of someone like Keith could be extraordinary.

We didn't try to streamline the ELP sound into deliberately short, radio-friendly tunes. The self-titled album's opening song, 'The Score', was a nine-minute piece that included a reference to the famous line from 'Karn Evil 9': *Welcome back, my friends, to the show that never ends* . . . Another song on the eight-track LP that topped the seven-minute mark was 'The Miracle', which remains a highlight for me. Also, we continued our tradition of combining rock and European classical music, and the album finished with our adaptation of the Holst piece 'Mars, the Bringer of War'. I had a fondness for this piece ever since we used to play it as an encore in King Crimson, and Cozy had a long relationship with it too. However, Keith was always wary of performing pieces of classical music that were too well known and so for a while we were in two minds whether to include this or not.

We still left room for a couple of radio-ready tracks, including 'Learning to Fly'. 'Touch and Go' was the first single from the album and it narrowly missed reaching the top forty in the United States – although it charted higher than some Emerson, Lake & Palmer songs even at our peak – while reaching number two on the rock radio chart.

Released in May 1986, the album went top forty on both sides of the Atlantic. It seemed that Emerson and Lake together had a bright future once again, along with Powell. Of course, some reviewers had their knives out as usual, and Cozy had a taste of what it's like when journalists just want to criticise you as individuals and don't even mention the music. I think he was shocked.

Highlights of our US tour included playing at Madison Square Garden again on 20 September 1986, which was recorded, and, for Keith, appearing on *Late Night with David Letterman*, where he played the Nice song, 'America', which we had incorporated into our live set along with some King Crimson songs.

Overall, though, the tour was badly handled by our US management at the time – it was not well coordinated and encountered various complications that were outside of the band's control. As 1986 drew to a close, we were losing momentum and shortly after the tour ended, so did Emerson, Lake & Powell.

Cozy was certainly a great player and I am proud of what we achieved together. I think that *Emerson, Lake & Powell* is a decent album – as well as 'The Miracle', 'Touch and Go' and 'The Score' seem to have stood the test of time and I still enjoy listening to them today – but the chemistry was never quite the same as it was in the original ELP. Even though the line-up with Carl Palmer had itself begun to lose its chemistry following the two *Works* albums, I look back on those early ELP recordings – *Emerson Lake & Palmer*, *Tarkus*, *Pictures at an Exhibition*, *Trilogy*, *Brain Salad Surgery* and *Welcome Back, My Friends* . . . – as the definitive era of ELP, and Carl was a huge part of that.

CHAPTER 15

Three Again

In 1991, Emerson, Lake and Palmer – the original trio – were invited to a lunch with an old friend of ours, Phil Carson. We knew Phil from way back when we were signed to Atlantic Records and he was running the company in Europe, and it was Phil who had the foresight to release 'I Believe in Father Christmas' as a single back in 1975.

At the meeting, Phil explained that he was about to form a new record company called Victory. He had teamed up with some Japanese investors who were interested in the possibility of becoming involved with Emerson, Lake & Palmer – there was an enduring love of the band in Japan ever since that amazing but crazy tour in 1972. The idea at the time was that we should possibly build on Keith's experience and pursue a film-score opportunity – which really meant creating a concept album for a movie. The idea of creating film soundtracks together as a band was completely new to us and seemed quite appealing.

Of course, you never know precisely when the right movie is going to come along so it was suggested that, in the meantime, we start writing and building up a reservoir of material that we could draw upon.

On the first day that we got together to rehearse, we stood by our instruments, getting ready to play. As usual, just in order to get everyone fired up, we decided to play through something familiar from the back catalogue. On this occasion, we chose 'Fanfare for the Common Man'. As we played, I instantly thought to myself just how special this band was in terms of its chemistry – we had such a powerful sound for only three players. We weren't always compatible as people, but as Carl recently said, 'When we played music together, it was the best time of our lives . . .'

People often talked about ELP having such a powerful sound for a trio, and other three-piece bands such as the Jimi Hendrix Experience, Cream and the Police were also able to create a lot of power. I think that this is because the human brain can only process up to perhaps three individual pathways of information – or types of sound – simultaneously. Beyond that you sometimes just hear a mass of sound, and the individual instruments can get lost in the ensemble. When it comes down just to three, you can still hear the full power of each individual source in equilibrium, without needing to diminish the sound of any one of them.

The rehearsals continued for some weeks, during which we began to develop quite a number of interesting ideas. Very soon it became obvious to everyone involved that we had enough material to form the basis of a completely new album. The question then was, do we wait until the right film comes our way or do we simply get on and record the songs that are ready to go?

In retrospect, I think that the whole idea that Phil Carson had put forward of ELP doing a film score was just a rather attractive carrot in order to get Carl, Keith and myself motivated to make another album together. In any event, it worked and there we were, just a few weeks later, with the backbone of a new Emerson, Lake & Palmer album ready to record.

The next question that arose was about who was going to produce the album. I had produced all of the early ELP recordings and each one of them had gone platinum, so I felt that the obvious thing was for us to repeat this successful formula, where I would sit in the chair but they would have their input too. It wasn't just ego – I thought it was a good way to help recapture the spirit of the early days. However, Keith and Carl did not want me to produce the record. They had worked together in 1988 in a band called 3, after the *Emerson, Lake & Powell* album – it hadn't worked out too well but perhaps they had got used to working together in a different way to the early ELP days. Whatever the reason, they insisted that we use an independent, outside producer. I certainly did not want anyone to feel obliged to have me produce the record so I immediately agreed that we should look elsewhere.

A short while after that, Phil Carson revealed that he had found someone in Los Angeles, whom he felt confident could handle the job. The person he suggested was Mark Mancina, who is now very well known as a composer of film scores but he had also worked with Trevor Rabin and Yes. It is, of course, a big thing for any artist to hand over the reins and put their trust in someone else. However, after meeting Mark and very quickly realising his extraordinary musical talent and warming to his endearing personality, I had every confidence that he could deliver a great recording.

Mark introduced us to his own recording engineer, Steve Kempster, who is in a class of his own. Together they formed a formidable team and were a real pleasure to work with. During the recording of what became *Black Moon*, Mark, Steve and I became extremely close friends, a friendship that, I am proud to say, endures to this very day.

I have always seen *Black Moon*, our eighth studio album, as unique. In some ways, it is not simply an ELP album; in truth, it is actually an ELPM album: Emerson, Lake, Palmer & Mancina. Such was the extraordinary contribution made by Mark.

After the band had left the studio to go home at night, Mark and Steve would stay behind and either play or replay a lot of the parts on the album themselves. The truth of the matter was that by the time *Black Moon* got made, the standard of playing inside ELP had deteriorated. On one occasion, I remember being in the studio together with Mark and Steve, just the three of us, recording my vocals. After a while, Mark came out of the control room, into the studio and walked over, very close to where I was standing, and quietly said, 'Tell me something, how did you do it?'

At first I really didn't understand and so I asked him what he meant.

He then said, 'Well, as a producer how did you manage to get the results you did on those early ELP recordings?'

He then went on to tell me, as diplomatically and respect-fully as he could, how surprised he was by the poor standard of playing and by the level of mistakes that were occurring. Mark was a really big fan of ELP during its formative years and I think he was probably a little disillusioned to find that the band he was now recording did not appear to have the same capabilities as it had done twenty years previously.

I explained to him that on those early recordings, apart from doing an intense amount of rehearsal beforehand, I did quite a lot of editing – much of the material for a track was recorded in relatively short bursts before finally being joined up as a single entity. Nonetheless, when we played the music live, the sound was great.

In spite of all the difficulties, Mark and indeed the whole band were determined to make a record of which we could all be proud. Listening back to it today, I must say that all things considered it is an outstanding record and deserves to take its place among the best of ELP, even if it did not really trouble the charts – the days of being in the top ten on both sides of the Atlantic were well and truly behind us.

All three of us, Keith, Carl and myself, co-wrote the 'Black Moon' title track, and my lyrics were inspired by the Gulf War and seeing the smoke from the oil wells black out the sun. We also all co-wrote 'Paper Blood', while Keith and I wrote 'Farewell to Arms' and 'Better Days'. I also contributed an acoustic ballad, 'Footprints in the Snow', and we included a section from Prokofiev's *Romeo and Juliet*. Mark wrote a song, 'Burning Bridges', specifically for the band. Keith's playing on 'Close to Home' shows that, even if some mistakes were being made in the studio, he was still a genuine keyboard virtuoso.

I wrote the single 'Affairs of the Heart' with Geoff Downes of Yes and Asia in the summer of 1988 when we were devising a project called *Ride the Tiger* that did not come to fruition. The six songs we wrote and performed together were finally released in 2015, although one of the songs, 'Love Under Fire', was recorded prior to then by Asia for their *Aqua* album in 1992.

Keith praised 'Affairs of the Heart', which had been inspired by a trip to Venice, as one of my best ever songs. He decided that the keyboard parts should be quite low-key to give space to my singing and guitar. I think we had all grown up a bit by then and appreciated each other's skills more rather than demanding attention for ourselves.

After the release of the *Black Moon* album on 27 June 1992, ELP undertook a worldwide tour and played three sold-out shows at the Royal Albert Hall in London, with Alan Freeman, who had always supported our music, introducing the first of them. It was over twenty years since the flag-burning incident at the Royal Albert Hall, so Keith's antics had been forgiven. The 3 October performance there was recorded for a live album released in 1993.

Although the tour was generally well received, and some people called the show 'high octane', I think by this time the cracks were beginning to show and the performances did not really match the quality or energy level that the band had been able to capture in its former years.

The next album we recorded was entitled *In the Hot Seat*, which we released on 27 September 1994. It was produced at the Goodnight LA Studios in Los Angeles by Keith Olsen, previously known for his work with Fleetwood Mac.

I have to be honest and say that for many years my perception of this album was one of it just being a complete failure. However, after listening back to the album, I can hear that, despite the chaos and confusion at the time, there are still some little jewels of creation that, had they happened under different circumstances, might very well have gone on to become a more important element of ELP's catalogue. 'Hand of Truth', 'One by One', 'Heart on

Ice' and 'Gone Too Soon' have some elements of the real ELP about them.

One good thing that did come out of the album was 'Daddy', which was written in memory of a young girl, Sara Anne Wood, who went missing in New York state; it was released as a charity single to raise money for the National Center for Missing & Exploited Children.

Unfortunately, things at the time were really not conducive to the making of a great record. Keith was starting to encounter problems with his ulnar nerve, which led to problems controlling his right hand and, from what we could gather, the prognosis for recovery did not look good. He was forced to overdub the right-hand parts with his left hand because of the problem. I think that it was around this time that Carl was having some trouble with carpal tunnel syndrome – a common problem for drummers – leading to numbness in his fingers, too, but unlike Keith's problem, it was remedied by an operation.

Unlike the *Black Moon* record we made with Mark Mancina, this album with Keith Olsen often felt to me as though it was being made purely for commercial reasons – I think Victory had lost money on other major bands' recent albums and they needed a hit. Olsen apparently told Keith that classical adaptations were no longer wanted, and there seemed to be some strange mix-up that meant that a version of Sibelius's *Karelia Suite* that we recorded remained unfinished and wasn't included on the album. You just have to look at the writing credits, many of which involve Keith Olsen and Bill Wray, to know that the three band members weren't really collectively driving the project. Of course, everyone loves to have success, but I have never felt comfortable with financial reward being the driving factor – after all, that's why my stint with Asia did not go very well. For me, success should come about as a by-product of being inspired by artistic values. Not that *In the Hot Seat* reaped any financial rewards anyway. It was our worst-selling album.

ELP continued to tour the world in the 1990s, but throughout this entire period I could feel inside of me that the band was not performing in the same way it had in its former years. Keith's hand condition was certainly one factor, but I also believe that the band was never really the same after the disintegration and splintering that took place during the *Works* period.

Although we never really spoke about it, I believe that both Keith and Carl had by now come to accept that not allowing me to continue producing the ELP records had probably been a mistake. Having said that, I think it is only right to point out that the dramatic drop in sales from our early records was in no way a reflection on the capability or the quality of the outside producers that were hired; it was simply a fact that by producing the early records in-house, we had stumbled on a formula that worked for us and, as the old saying goes, if it ain't broke, don't fix it.

In the Hot Seat, our ninth studio album, was our last.

CHAPTER 16

A Starr and a Crusader

In 2001, I had just returned home one day after walking my dog, a Dalmatian called Astor, in Richmond Park in London when the phone rang. I picked up the receiver and immediately recognised the voice at the other end.

It was Ringo Starr. He wanted me to join his group, the All-Starr Band.

Although he and I had never met before, it immediately felt as if I was talking to someone I had known all my life. The first thing that struck me was how down to earth and humble he was. I'm sure most people would agree that the Beatles were the biggest rock band in the world, and that they changed our cultural heritage through the power of their music. Elvis Presley and Bob Dylan are perhaps two others that, to me, deserve a similar kind of recognition.

One of the things I came to understand about Ringo, which

I had not fully realised before we worked together, was just how important he was to the success of the Beatles. As a musician, I personally find his drumming mesmerising. If you listen to any Beatles recording and focus on the drum part, you will hear that it is simply flawless. Ringo always did the right thing at the right time, never too little and never too much, never self-indulgent and always uplifting, empowering the music to do its work.

Apart from good musicianship, the other thing that really makes a great band is chemistry. It is simply this cocktail of personality, energy, karma, call it what you will, that when mixed together in the right way becomes effervescent, perhaps even explosive. Ringo's contribution to the Beatles in this respect was enormous.

You will often hear people talking about a drummer in terms of feel. Ringo sometimes describes his own feel as being laid-back and perhaps just slightly on the back end of the beat, and I think this is pretty near the truth. The other thing is, of course, consistency: that feeling of reliability you get when playing with a drummer who has this gift of feel means that you can almost switch to autopilot and then just sit back and enjoy the ride. That is the feeling you get when playing with Ringo.

Rehearsals for the Ringo Starr & His New All-Starr Band tour took place at the Niagara Fallsview Casino in Canada. The first thing I wanted to do when I arrived was to make sure that all my guitars and equipment were in good shape and ready to go, so I made my way over to the rehearsal room to take a look. When I walked in, the whole place was already buzzing with activity so I decided to just take a quick peek and maybe come back a bit later when things had settled down.

Before I turned to leave, I briefly picked up my bass and strolled back to adjust my amplifier when I suddenly realised that Sheila E. – known for her work with Prince as well as her own solo work – was already sitting there behind her drum kit. We smiled and said a quick hello and I played a few lines on my bass. All of sudden, I felt the sound of thunder strike me right in the middle of my back just as if I'd been hit by a train. Sheila had started to play along with the bass and the power she generated was truly formidable. Any reservations I might have previously had about female drummers not being powerful enough were instantly eradicated. Apart from being a lovely, spiritual person, Sheila is a masterful musician.

The next person to come in to the room was Howard Jones. Of course, I was already familiar with Howard's music. I might not have liked all new music in the 1980s, but I always thought Howard had an extraordinary and unusual songwriting talent and I had enjoyed watching him perform back in the UK.

Just as Howard began to settle on to his keyboards, into the room came Roger Hodgson of Supertramp. Although we had never met before, I could immediately sense that Roger was a gentle and spiritual soul who really communicated through his songs and his love for music. Of course, I was aware of the enormous success of Supertramp and was certainly looking forward to having the chance of playing with him in concert on a few of the songs he had composed – 'The Logical Song', 'Give a Little Bit' and 'Take the Long Way Home'.

The next person to arrive was Ian Hunter, the former lead singer of Mott the Hoople. Ian really is a larger-than-life character and it did not take long to also discover what a down-to-earth guy he is. He is a great songwriter who lives for rock and roll. Although quite uncompromising where his music is concerned, he is an extremely likeable and generous person, and we became really good friends as the tour went along.

Next to arrive was the musical director Mark Rivera. Apart from being an MD, Mark is an extremely talented multi-instrumentalist. His main instrument is the saxophone and some of his solos are truly breathtaking. He is in demand from some the world's great artists such as Elton John, Paul Simon and Bruce Springsteen, and has been playing in Billy Joel's band for thirty-five years. Again, quite apart from being a first-class musician, Mark is also an extremely charming person with an infectious smile.

Well, there we were, all assembled and ready to go, none of us having played together before and no one knowing quite what to expect. Very soon, Ringo arrived and we began to work through the set. I think everyone there was quite thrilled at how good the band sounded. Having two drummers

252

certainly made the whole thing very strong rhythmically and there was an unmistakable joy in the music – and that lasted throughout the two-month tour. We only rehearsed for ten days and put together a two-and-a-half-hour show, which was a great achievement as most of us had never performed any of each other's music before.

The set consisted of Beatles and Ringo Starr songs, which were great fun to play, alongside a selection of songs from each of the different band members, so we played 'The Court of the Crimson King', 'Karn Evil 9: 1st Impression – Part 2' and 'Lucky Man'. The version of 'Lucky Man' was captured on the 2002 live album *King Biscuit Flower Hour Presents Ringo and His New All-Starr Band*.

One of the many fond memories that I took away from that tour was when we travelled after the show. As soon as we had finished the last song, we would immediately rush out and get into the waiting cars. Invariably we would have a police escort that took us directly to the airport. It was always amusing to see how the motorcycle cops used to love riding up alongside the car and giving Ringo a thumbs up or a wave. Upon our arrival at the airport we would board the jet and take off pretty much immediately. As soon as we got up to cruising altitude, everyone would then unbuckle their seat belts and begin chatting.

Most nights Ringo and all the band would sit together and we would listen to him tell stories. Everyone was interested in hearing about the Beatles, of course, and we were given many fascinating insights into their life together as a band. However, I think Ringo had been asked so many questions about the Beatles during his lifetime that he would far prefer to reflect on the period before the Beatles, when rock and roll was in its infancy. Another thing that I found really interesting was that, due to the fact that he was in the band himself, he never got to experience the Beatles in the same way that everyone else did. He was inside that very small bubble looking out while the whole world was looking in.

That tour with Ringo and His All-Starr Band was one of the most enjoyable I had ever been on. The people were great, the music was great and Ringo really is a star.

A couple of years later, on 22 June 2003, I was invited to attend the wedding of James Sellar, the son of a long-standing friend, Irvine Sellar, best known among other things for having built the remarkable Shard skyscraper in London. Irvine and I had originally met through our daughters, who attended the same school in Surrey, and I had known James from back when he was just a small boy.

The wedding was taking place at Cliveden House in Buckinghamshire. Cliveden is more of a palace than it is a house, with spectacular landscaped views overlooking the River Thames. It became particularly notorious during the late 1960s as it was often used as a discreet place where politicians would entertain their weekend girlfriends, and also as the setting for what is now referred to as the Profumo affair. Apart from its history, the whole setting is truly breathtaking.

All the guests checked in to their rooms, and then we began to assemble out on the grand terrace for drinks. After a short while, Irvine came over to me and said, 'I have someone here I think you might like to meet. He's a musician just like you.'

The musician was, in fact, Richard Desmond, the owner of the Northern & Shell publishing group, which owns the *Daily Express*, the *Daily Star, OK!* magazine and Channel 5.

After we shook hands, Richard told me that, contrary to most people's perception of him, his first love is music. He began playing drums during his early teenage years and had originally intended for that to become his career. He couldn't make enough money as a drummer and he was unable to pay his mother the rent they had agreed upon, so she basically forced him to go out and earn some money. He started selling advertising in small trade magazines, and that was the beginning of his phenomenally successful career in publishing.

Richard continued: 'I still enjoy playing the drums when I can and I'm actually putting together a band with Roger Daltrey to raise money for charity. We were wondering if you would like to be involved? The band will be called the RD Crusaders.'

Apart from my involvement in supporting animal shelters and campaigning for the National Center for Missing & Exploited Children in the United States, it had been quite a while since I had been involved in charity work so I willingly agreed.

Apart from Richard, Roger and myself, over the years the varied line-up has included Robert Plant; Lulu; my friend Gary Moore; Steve Smith, the drummer from Journey; Rick Wills, the bassist with Foreigner; Gary Brooker of Procol Harum; and Simon Townshend, the brother of Pete, who has performed with the Who and Pearl Jam.

One of the mainstays of the Crusaders is Russ Ballard. A terrific guy, Russ was the lead singer of Argent back in the 1970s, and as a songwriter has penned hits for Rainbow, Kiss, Santana, Roger Daltrey and many more. His knowledge of rock-and-roll history is remarkable. Another regular is the keyboardist George 'Zoot' Money. He began his career in Bournemouth, very near to where I started my own career, and in the early days during the 1960s we would often appear at the same clubs and dance venues. Zoot, who has played with a whole roster of people including Spencer Davis and the Animals, has soul music running through his veins and anyone into that music should definitely go and see him perform.

The very first RD Crusaders show took place in September 2003 at Ronnie Scott's jazz club in London in aid of Teenage Cancer Trust. For some weeks before the show, Richard and I would get together at his house in London and rehearse through the material. It's a strange thing how music brings people together but over those weeks and months we spent rehearsing, Richard and I developed a close friendship that remains until this day. I was truly honoured to have been part of the Crusaders for a while.

All the Crusaders shows were fun and, of course, what really made them gratifying was the amount of money they generated for charity – over £14 million so far. The material we performed was a mixture of the best-known songs from each of the band members, with the backbone of the show being mainly material from the Who's back catalogue. Playing the Who songs was particularly enjoyable for me, firstly because they are all great compositions but, perhaps even more importantly, also because Roger is such a pivotal part of the Who sound and of their remarkable history.

One thing that I soon noticed about Roger is that his hearing has become so sensitive. If a pop went off a lead, he would jump. You would think after years and years of being in the Who, one of the loudest bands going, he would be immune or even deaf to loud noises, but almost any noise makes him jump.

I remember getting a call from Roger a few days after one of the shows, asking me if I would like to record with the Who. I believe their regular bass player Pino Palladino, who started playing for them after John Entwistle sadly passed away in 2002, was unable to make it for some reason and so Roger had suggested to Pete Townshend that it might be a good idea to try and get me in.

Roger also told me that Zak Starkey would be playing drums during the session, which was great news as I am a big fan of Zak's playing. It really was great fun working together with him after touring with his father, Ringo, and it was very interesting to see both the similarities and the differences in the way that they perform. The one thing that immediately struck me was that they share this remarkable gift of feel, and also the ability to know when it is better to leave a space rather than simply to keep blasting through the tune, filling every possible bar with noise.

The song we recorded at Eel Pie studios in Twickenham was called 'Real Good Looking Boy', written by Pete Townshend and partly inspired by the story of Elvis Presley. Roger, like me, saw Elvis play live when he was young and was truly inspired by him.

Although I was more than familiar with the recordings of the Who, it was not until I got in the same room and played with them that I began to add up all the dots and understand what really made them tick.

Of course, everyone is aware that Pete is an extremely talented songwriter, but I do sometimes get the impression that he is not given the full credit he deserves for being the great guitar player that he is. The reason for this, I think, is that Pete's guitar-playing forms a very supportive role in the Who's overall sound, and many of his guitar parts work on two levels simultaneously and seamlessly, i.e. part rhythm and part lead, all bound up into one powerful package. The way he uses punctuation and staccato is simply unsurpassed and for me that is what makes his style of playing so unique.

'Real Good Looking Boy' was recorded in one take and, although perhaps not a typical Who song, it did nevertheless bear the hallmark that all of the band's recordings have, which is the inescapable identity of Pete's guitar-playing and Roger's voice. When you consider that, added to this formidable combination, before they both passed away the Who also had the benefit of Keith Moon's drumming and John Entwistle's bass-playing, it is little wonder they achieved the iconic status that they have.

I was delighted when 'Real Good Looking Boy' was put on the Who's compilation album *Here and Now* in 2004, rubbing shoulders with the classics 'I Can't Explain', 'My Generation', 'Pinball Wizard' and all the others. I am proud to have played a tiny part in the Who legend.

I seem to have always been lucky when it came to forming bands and, as a result, I've had the good fortune to have worked together with some of the world's truly great players. The Greg Lake Band was no exception.

The band was formed in 2005 for a tour of the United Kingdom. It consisted of Brett Morgan, who has drummed for everyone from George Harrison to Sting, Trevor Barry on bass, and Florian Opahle, who has worked a lot with Ian Anderson of Jethro Tull, on guitar. Dave Arch was the acting MD and on keyboards. Many British television viewers will know Dave's name as he is the MD on BBC1's *Strictly Come Dancing*, but as a keyboardist he has worked on hundreds of film scores, including the Harry Potter series, and he has recorded for everyone from Philip Glass to Paul McCartney to the Spice Girls. Dave helped me to shape new live interpretations of the ELP classics 'Fanfare for the Common Man' and 'Pictures at an Exhibition'.

I can only say that this is the sort of band that one dreams about forming – musicians of the very highest calibre with personalities to match. In some ways, I suppose you could compare it to driving a really powerful Bentley with automatic drive. The whole thing just floats along effortlessly as it generates a seemingly endless and awesome amount of power.

I have to say that despite the fact that we were only together for a very short time, playing with these people was one of the most rewarding musical experiences of my entire career. Ten years after the band was formed, we met up for lunch to celebrate this special anniversary. This band meant a lot to all of us and, indeed, Florian flew all the way from Munich to London just for the occasion. It was a moving moment, all being together once again and sitting around one table.

Thankfully the 2005 tour, which also featured '21st Century Schizoid Man', 'Touch and Go', 'In the Court of the Crimson King' and 'Lucky Man' on the set list, was recorded for the DVD and album *Greg Lake: Live*. It really would have been more honest to call it *Greg Lake, Dave Arch, Trevor Barry, Brett Morgan and Florian Opahle: Live*.

■ ■ ■

In 2006 and 2007, I appeared in the United States as a guest with the Trans-Siberian Orchestra on some of their Christmas extravaganzas. The TSO concept is as remarkable as it is unlikely. The whole thing was conceived by Paul O'Neill together with long-standing friend and musical arranger and producer Robert Kinkel, along with Jon Oliva and Al Pitrelli, who are both members of the heavy rock band Savatage.

It turns out that Paul and Robert are big Emerson, Lake & Palmer fans, and one day in the 1990s they came up with the idea of doing a 'progressive rock' Christmas show. I think the idea was to use classically influenced rock music as a basis for the show. After crystallising the whole concept, they then went to almost every promoter in the United States to try and get the whole thing off the ground. Without exception, each and every one of them turned the band down (something that is slightly reminiscent of the Beatles story).

Eventually, after having exhausted every other possibility, they managed to persuade one of their friends, a small concert promoter in Cleveland, Ohio, to put on the first small show. After doing everything humanly possible to sell tickets, the show went ahead and to everyone's surprise it was well received.

The following year they asked the same promoter if he would be prepared to do the same show again but this time in a slightly larger venue. Again, he was reluctant and, again, tried to dissuade them from doing it. However, as before, they managed to persuade him to do it and the show went ahead, this time selling out surprisingly fast.

Since then, year upon year the whole TSO concept has become a phenomenon, selling out every night during the month of December in arenas on the East and West Coasts. The shows are multi-media events with anything up to fifty singers and musicians, including a string section, performing on stage at any given time, accompanied by lasers, a light show, video screens and moving elements of the stage, all synchronised to the music. By the time I linked up with them, the band had released a series of Christmas-related rock-opera albums, *Christmas Eve and Other Stories* (1996), *The Christmas Attic* (1998) and *The Lost Christmas Eve* (2004), and they have now sold over ten million albums.

They donate a dollar to local and national charities for every ticket sold on their tours, raising over $10 million, particularly for charities that help children. Classically influenced music, technologically advanced stage shows, a love of Christmas and a concern for child welfare – they are a band after my own heart, and it was a pleasure to perform with them. Apart from all this, Paul O'Neill and I discovered that we had something else in common, which was that we both love to collect books and are both extremely interested in history. Perhaps this is part of the reason why we both feel a connection to classical music.

We performed 'Karn Evil 9' together at the 2006 and 2007 concerts. Then, in 2009, Trans-Siberian Orchestra recorded 'Nutrocker', which had always been a favourite of ELP live performances, for their album *Night Castle*. I was touched that the TSO asked me to play bass on their recording, and I was honoured to accept. The album has sold over a million copies in the United States.

CHAPTER 17

A High Voltage Finale

In 2009 Keith Emerson and I decided to write together again. During the day, we would take a short break and play old Emerson, Lake & Palmer songs just for fun. We noticed that when it was just the two of us playing, the songs had a different feeling than we were used to. Over all of these years, we had played them live in the band and had heard the albums hundreds of times, but of course, when we wrote most of that early material, it was often just the two of us working on the songs. When we played those songs for fun in 2009, it took us right back to the roots of the songs, before they were augmented with other instruments, produced and mixed. The sound was quite different, and we heard the material conceptually again. We thought that was an interesting new perspective on the material.

We then had the idea of creating a show that would offer the audience an insight on how these songs had evolved, with the two of us performing them. I am not sure that Carl would have wanted to be involved, but he had commitments to Asia in any case.

We set the stage up to look like a recording studio with an engineer behind the mixing desk – the engineer was Keith Wechsler, who has worked with us for a long time. He would issue the instructions and then the red light would go on 'Record', and then we would start the show. Inspired by our old label, Manticore, we created a fantasy of what Manticore Hall would look like. Whenever ELP or even just E & L got together, the production would turn out to be expensive.

The rehearsals for the 'Manticore Hall' tour took place inside an aircraft hangar on the Santa Monica airfield in California. Keith worked around the difficulties with his hand, but, although the music was developing well, I noticed that there was something strange about the way he was behaving. He became increasingly reluctant to arrive at rehearsals on time, and the start times got later and later. The tour was looming and ideally we would have postponed it. However, it was too late to cancel it without causing significant problems.

The first show was due to be performed at the Civic Auditorium in Lakewood, Cleveland, Ohio, on 1 April 2010 and we set up at the venue the day before to rehearse. Due to technical issues, it was early evening before we got under way. We played for a couple of hours and I decided to go backstage for a coffee break. After sitting there for a few minutes, I looked up and saw Keith walking towards me with tears streaming down his face.

'I'm really sorry, Greg, but I can't go on,' he said.

At first, I didn't know what to say but as soon as I had collected my thoughts I realised that the best thing to do was to get him back to the hotel. Maybe he would feel better after a rest.

On the next afternoon, I arrived at the venue for the sound check. Keith arrived later, at around five o'clock, and came on stage to start preparing his equipment. I could immediately see that his face looked ashen and drawn, and it was clear that he had not slept well. We started to run through the material and make the necessary adjustments. In the middle of this, at 6.30, the doors to the venue were opened, despite the fact that we had warned the promoter to keep them closed. The audience started to drift into the theatre, so we decided to head back to the dressing room and wait for show time.

After a few minutes, the tour manager came into the dressing room.

'Has anyone seen Keith?' he asked.

We went outside to look for him but he was nowhere to be seen. Eventually one of the security staff said that he had seen Keith leaving by the back door of the theatre and jumping into a taxi.

We waited for him to return, but given the way Keith had seemed over the last couple of days, we knew he was not suddenly going to reappear, having popped back to the hotel for something he had forgotten. It became obvious to all concerned that the show was not going to take place.

The announcement was made to the audience shortly thereafter. It was April Fool's day, but it was no joke: the concert had to be cancelled forty minutes after the scheduled start time. I attributed Keith's behaviour to stage fright but he would later deny this. He said he merely had no time to tune up his Moog.

We decided it would be best to cancel the next couple of shows to try and allow Keith time to get back on track. Happily, it worked. Keith returned in good shape and the tour was able to continue. We started to really enjoy the performances. We did King Crimson's 'I Talk to the Wind' from *In the Court of the Crimson King* because I had never performed it live before, as well as the Nice's 'America' and 'Rondo'. We had unearthed some other surprises while we were putting together the set list, such as the fact that 'Bitches Crystal' from *Tarkus* was very interesting to play as a duo. It's such a rhythmic piece that we thought it wouldn't work without a drummer, but it did. We also played 'Pirates', 'Lucky Man', 'The Barbarian', 'Take a Pebble', 'Tarkus', 'From the Beginning' and 'C'est la Vie' among others, all of which can be heard on the live album we released, *Live from Manticore Hall*, so the set covered different aspects of our work together.

Some songs featured sequenced backing tracks, but on many it was just the two of us playing together – nothing else. Sometimes we could wander off the script and go where the music took us. This was one of the things that King Crimson would do. One of the tenets of the band was that it was just as important to listen to your bandmates as it was to play, so I had acquired that skill.

It was an adventure to put the Emerson & Lake 'Manticore Hall' show together, and so gratifying to see that the material still held up and we were receiving standing ovations. There was a strong sense of family, not just between myself and Keith, but with the audience during those performances.

While we were preparing for 'Manticore Hall', we received an offer for Emerson, Lake & Palmer to perform at the High Voltage Festival in Victoria Park, London, in summer 2010. We spoke to Carl and the three of us realised that this might be the last time the band would be able to perform live. So we agreed to do it.

The rehearsals took place at Shepperton Film Studios just outside London. It was surreal hearing us perform together again after so many years apart. It was as if someone had edited out twelve years of my life and joined the two ends up together. Frankly, it took a lot of energy and determination to reach a playing standard that people expected from a band like ELP. People were coming to see the legendary ELP. What did they expect? I'll tell you. They expected to see the band they heard on record or saw on tour in 1974. And now, decades older, we had to do it the same way. That took some doing. Carl went on record to say that he could not understand why we needed to rehearse for weeks before the show, but he later admitted that maybe that wasn't long enough.

The atmosphere was not helped when Carl told the media that he had expected us to be at each other's throats again. I have never understood his negative tendency. Keith and I had come to treasure and value each other, despite our differences over the years. We were getting on better than we ever had done. But I think that Carl found it harder to let go of the grudges from the past, and sadly for him it's always the person carrying the grudge that bears the burden. I have always liked Carl, whatever our differences, but there wasn't much I could do about it.

We appeared on the main stage of the High Voltage Festival on Sunday 25 July 2010, almost exactly forty years after we had first performed together. Gary Moore had played the day before, and Ian Hunter, who I had got to know on the tour with Ringo, was also on the bill on the main stage on Sunday.

We played some of the works our fans loved the most – including 'Karn Evil 9: 1st Impression Part 2', 'Tarkus' and 'Pictures at an Exhibition', finishing with a medley involving 'Fanfare for the Common Man'. Despite various technical problems, the ELP show was an intensely emotional and nostalgic experience for the three of us, and for the people who came along that night. Many of them had been there with us since the early 1970s. Afterwards, the atmosphere backstage was like a cross between a party and a funeral. There were people with tears in their eyes and others celebrating with champagne – and some with both.

Having done the work and preparation to bring the band up to touring speed, I was keen for us to take the show around the world one last time. It would be a final thank you to our fans. My own philosophy of music has always been that I'm only here because a lot of people were good enough to buy my records and the records of ELP. I feel a sense of duty to play or perform that music for those people. However, Carl didn't want to continue and the idea was dropped. It frustrated me. We had only done the one show, and after five or six more the band might have been formidable again. Carl saw it differently, and even Keith was reluctant. I don't know why. It was very strange, but there was something about ELP that did not work any more in terms of a brotherhood. It used to work, but it didn't work now.

The High Voltage show was the last time ELP ever performed.

CHAPTER 18

Songs of a Lifetime

After Emerson, Lake & Palmer had come to an end, I still felt that there was some part of me as an artist that remained unresolved. I think that it was perhaps a sense of not having had the chance to say goodbye to the long-standing fans of my music with ELP and with King Crimson. The idea that I came up with was for a show that would be an intimate, shared experience in which the audience and I could reflect on some of the songs, memories and moments that we have shared together over the years. I decided to play not only King Crimson, ELP and my solo songs, but also include music that influenced me when I was growing up. I played Elvis's 'Heartbreak Hotel', the Beatles's 'You've Got to Hide Your Love Away' and a few songs that may have surprised people a little, such as Curtis Mayfield's 'People Get Ready'. I called the tour, which took place in 2012, 'Songs of a Lifetime'.

Apart from performing the music – solo – I would also invite members of the audience to offer up memories that they would like to share, so the whole event became more like a family gathering than a rock concert. This linked right back to the start of my career, when Dee Anthony told me that I should always sing as if I was singing to just one person, to make that individual, emotional connection. I always tried to make sure that I was communicating in a direct, heartfelt and meaningful way. The letters I received from people over the years told me that I had entered their lives in a personal way, and it was good to hear some of their stories in person.

I have to say that, before the tour began, I was a little nervous about how the audience would respond to that kind of unusual format but, after the first night, I was completely reassured that it was going to work. It really is all about human nature: people love to hear stories being told and they also like to tell stories themselves. They love to reflect on their youth and listen to the music that was so important to them during their formative years, and it is wonderful to do that with people who have had similar experiences.

During the tour, one thing that took me by complete surprise was just how many incredible stories the audience had to offer. Every night, some of the stories would cause the audience to laugh uproariously or cry, or both – and all of this together with the music made for a really entertaining evening. Although I missed the company and comradeship of having a band on tour with me, it was more than compensated for by the participation of the audience.

Before the tour began, a number of people tried to dissuade me from doing it on the basis that a one-man show would not be sufficient to entertain an audience for a full two hours. How wrong they were! Most nights after the show had finished, I went out to sign autographs and so on, and was often still there until way past midnight listening to the recollections and experiences that people wanted to share with me. This tour really did prove to be a lesson in human nature and I will always be proud and grateful that I was able to do it. We toured 'Songs of a Lifetime' all around the United States and Canada as well as the UK and Europe.

One outstanding memory I have of performing this show in Europe was on 28 November 2012 in the small city of Piacenza in Italy. The concert took place at a wonderful theatre there, the Teatro Municipale, which looks rather like La Scala in Milan with beautiful gold balconies and crystal chandeliers. I love Piacenza, and the Conservatorio di Musica Giuseppe Nicolini there awarded me an honorary degree in 2016 for the way that King Crimson and Emerson, Lake & Palmer helped to bring classical music into young people's lives – what an honour.

The show at Teatro Municipale was recorded and I decided to release a special collectors' edition of it on vinyl. Somehow the event, the feeling of the music and the atmosphere all seem to be suited to being reproduced in this analogue way.

Max Marchini recorded and produced the concert in Piacenza, and together with Max I decided to restore the Manticore Records label for the production and distribution of high-quality vinyl recordings.

For most of my life I have been performing in stadiums, arenas, festivals or large theatres, and one thing that I really came to enjoy on this 'Songs of a Lifetime' tour was being able to get really close to the audience on a one-to-one basis and see how the music I made throughout my life had somehow reached out and become attached to their lives. For any artist, I think this is one of the most gratifying things to experience.

On 11 March 2016, I received a phone call from one of my managers with the dreadful news that Keith Emerson had been found dead at his house in Santa Monica; he had apparently committed suicide with a self-inflicted gunshot to the head.

This tragic news came as a shock at the time, but I have to say that it really did not come as a complete surprise. All of us who were close to Keith knew that he was quite a troubled soul who would periodically fall into deep bouts of depression and was often overcome with feelings of self-doubt. This in turn often resulted in him resorting to self-medication in one form or another.

It is natural that people are interested in knowing how and why this tragedy happened in the way that it did, and as someone who was extremely close to Keith for many years, and whose lives were so entwined, I am constantly being asked about what I believe was the cause.

It is always easy to point to the usual suspects such as alcohol abuse, prescription drugs, and so on, but I believe that in most cases these are merely symptoms of what invariably lies somewhere far deeper below the surface.

In Keith's case, some people speculated on the cause being a feeling of despair about the progressive muscle degeneration taking place in his right arm, which in turn caused him to start losing control of the fingers of his right hand. Although this may have been a contributing factor, the problem with his right arm started as far back as the ELP recording of *In the Hot Seat* in 1994. He had lived with the problem for over two decades, so the theory that this is what suddenly caused him to take his own life does not really sound plausible to me.

It should also be borne in mind that by the time of Keith's death, he was seventy-one years old, so it would have been more than reasonable for him to retire at that point with both dignity and respect intact – without the arm causing him any further issues when performing live.

The other theory that was put forward was that Keith's actions were due to a few people writing derogatory remarks about his playing. Both Keith and I have lived all of our lives in the public eye, and have often found ourselves the target of insults and criticism from almost every imaginable quarter. I doubt very much if one or two instances in themselves, so late in life, would have been sufficient to have caused such a tragic reaction.

That being said, I did notice in recent years that Keith had become increasingly drawn to the internet, focusing more and more upon the opinions of a few isolated people who were posting not always pleasant comments there, and then viewing these as being representative of general opinion. Most of the time, of course, their opinions were a very long way from the truth.

I remember trying to explain to Keith on more than one occasion that, more often than not, the people who post these provocative or negative comments simply have nothing better to do with their lives than to sit up all night staring at a laptop, trying to find something provocative or controversial to say.

In any event, I just do not believe these few negative comments alone would have been sufficient to push him over the edge. I personally feel sure there was something far deeper taking place, something perhaps that he felt unable to deal with or escape from.

A few years ago, Keith and I were round at my house in Richmond doing some writing together, and I asked him what he considered to be the source of his musical inspiration and imagination. He then explained to me that he grew up as an only child and that his family lived on the third or fourth floor of an apartment building. His bedroom window looked directly over a small grass area where all the children from the building would congregate and play. For some reason, Keith's mother refused to allow him to go outside and play with the other children and, as a result, for a number of years he was more or less confined to his own bedroom.

I detected a slight quivering in his voice as he went on to tell me that sometimes when he was alone, he could still hear the voices of the children in his head, laughing and playing and having fun, and he would remember how alone he felt.

When I asked him if he thought this had affected him, his answer was that being alone in his room for such a long time had prompted him to live in a world of his own creation. In effect, this became the imaginary world of Keith Emerson, a world he would later visit to inspire the music he made – his incredible, ground-breaking creativity was partly born out of a desire to try to shut out the sense of isolation.

There were two distinct sides to Keith's personality, one very light, laughing and joking, and almost childlike, and another rather dark and fearful soul from a distant world that would suddenly appear. The difference between the two was almost impossible to reconcile.

Keith's life came to a tragic end and no one will ever know for sure what actually brought it about, but I cannot help but wonder if the loneliness of that little boy in his bedroom somehow came back to haunt him in his later life.

None of us on this earth are in total control of our own destiny and, in many respects, we are all bound to play the hand we have been dealt. During the many years Keith and I worked together, there were some days that were very difficult. Such is the nature of emotional or mental problems. We all have our own problems and we all have our own demons.

Whatever our occasional disagreements, the Keith Emerson I will always remember lives in the genius of the music he created and in his ability to make musical instruments such as the Hammond organ and Moog synthesiser talk as if they were human. Keith was a true master of his art.

Death is life.

This was the concept and indeed the final line of 'Pictures at an Exhibition'. I am not really a religious person and do not subscribe to any form of organised religion. That is not to say that I deny that there is any form of supreme creative being. I personally believe that, if there is a God, then for me I see this most clearly manifested in the nature that surrounds us. Whenever I go into a forest or walk by the side of a river, I always marvel at the beauty and complexity that exists there. Surely this is not something that could have possibly been created by the hand of man.

When I stare into the sky at night and look at the galaxy, and try to consider for a moment the meaning of infinity, I cannot help but wonder what lies out there beyond the stars.

I believe that life is perhaps like a circle: there is no beginning and there is no end, it simply continues to transform and evolve.

Ever since my late teens I have always been fascinated by the purpose and meaning of life and have always been interested in the philosophical writings of people like Khalil Gibran. I'm pretty sure this inquisitive instinct came from my mother, who herself was always interested in wise insights into life and beyond.

Of course, everyone is entitled to his or her own beliefs, and no one should have the right to force anyone else to accept theirs. Far too many wars and too much suffering have been caused by religious fanaticism. I see religious bigotry as being a very long way from the notion of what people generally think of when they think of God.

Personally, I believe the world would be a far better place if religion were kept strictly as a personal and private matter. Live and let live is what I say.

On the subject of life and death, I was recently diagnosed with terminal pancreatic cancer and told that this has spread to other parts of my body. Unfortunately, surgery is no longer an option. Needless to say, a moment such as this will give anyone good reason to reflect on their own beliefs.

I think most people live with some sort of feeling of foreboding about the terrible day when they will be told that they are going to die. However, the strangest thing was that on the day I was told, the sense of fear and dread that I had always expected never came. I believe the reason for this is probably due to my belief in the power of nature and my acceptance that death is simply a part of life. No one cries when the leaves fall from the trees because they know that in the spring new leaves will come again.

My life has been blessed in far too many ways to count. I have a wonderful family, a small number of really close friends, and have lived a life in music that I could never have even dreamed about as a young child. Just before I was diagnosed, I also received the gift of a wonderful grandson, Gabriel, and so there is nothing more I could possibly wish for.

I would just like to take this opportunity to thank all those people, colleagues, fans, family and friends, who have supported me over the years. Without your love and encouragement, the life I have lived would never have been possible.

I have been a lucky man.

By Stewart Young

Greg Lake passed away, aged sixty-nine, on 7 December 2016. At his funeral service on 20 December, his manager Stewart Young gave this eulogy.

Welcome Back, My Friends

My father introduced me to Greg forty-five years ago. He was twenty-three, I was twenty-five.

He was charismatic, warm and a rock star.

I was wearing a three-piece suit with matching shirt and tie and was a chartered accountant. I worked with ELP for a few months ... then they asked me to manage them. I was unsure. I met with Greg and told him that I knew nothing about the music business ... he replied, 'Nobody does – you can always talk to me.'

From that moment we became fast friends and spent many a magical evening during which Greg would play music, tell stories about the business, and advise me who I had to meet.

I learned so much in those days. Greg was always pushing the envelope: to make things beautiful; to aim for the top.

My life changed.

The next few years were wondrous. ELP reached heights that we could never have dreamed of. It was an exciting ride. We conquered the world.

Just when you thought life could not get any better for Greg, he met the love of his life, Regina. I had the honour to be his best man, and then along came his daughter, Natasha.

When the band were recording in the Bahamas we bought a house together and lived as one family, with Jimmy the parrot and Strawberry the dog.

Greg loved the countryside and when ELP were recording in Montreux, we went to the local bicycle store. Naturally, Greg bought the best bike ... a Tour de France special. I bought the second best. The owner, Mr Rochat, took us out for a trial spin. The sun was out, it was beautiful ... until we came to a steep hill. Both Greg and I were not as fit as we thought and Mr Rochat had to push me up the hill by my backside. We decided to keep the bikes in the studio in the valley down by the lake and every now and then used to ride to Evian for lunch. Greg really loved these rides and years later we would reminisce about them.

In February 2014, Greg called to share with me that he had just been diagnosed with terminal pancreatic cancer. He told me he had no regrets. Coming from a humble background, he had gone on to a life he could never have imagined – he had fulfilled every ambition, bought anything he wanted, but what really matters is love in your life, and he'd been blessed with Regina, Natasha, and now he had a grandson, Gabriel.

I saw Greg six months later, after he had finished the first part of his chemo. We were meeting for lunch, and when I looked across the room I couldn't see him. Suddenly I saw a hand waving and it was Greg. He had lost an enormous amount of weight, but it was still Greg. He had a twinkle in his eyes and said, 'I don't look too bad – we use to spend thousands in the old days to go to Champneys to lose weight.' On one of our visits to Champneys, we escaped during the night and went to a petrol station and bought their whole supply of Mars bars, and left the wrappers outside some of the other guests' rooms.

We would speak on the phone and have lunch whenever he felt well enough. One day he called and asked if I fancied Japanese and told me he would bring his little friend. That was when I first met his grandson, Gabriel. What a great lunch.

Inevitably Greg's health started to go downhill and he became bedbound, so I saw him at home.

Regina took care of him incredibly well. At this stage, Greg couldn't eat, but he still made sure I was fed and champagne was on hand. The three of us toasted.

He had not lost his sense of humour. He looked at me and said, 'You corrupted me. The first time you took me out for lunch we went to the White Elephant and you ordered a bottle of Bâtard-Montrachet.'

This was his introduction to the good life.

I guess he changed me. I changed him.

In the end the pain was too great and he had to go to a hospice. I visited him twice and, although he was very ill, we had a ball.

The last time I saw him I brought my sound system and played him a mix of a new version he had recorded of 'Closer to Believing'. When it started playing I was worried it was too loud . . . I asked Greg should I turn it down. He said, 'No, it's only 4.30, turn it up . . .'

Towards the end, Greg asked Regina to get him some caviar. Not just any caviar . . . Beluga. The last solid thing he ate was a few spoons of Beluga.

Greg decided he had to get Gabriel a bicycle for Christmas. It couldn't be just any bicycle . . . it had to be the best. On Greg's last weekend, Regina brought a Christmas tree and Natasha brought Gabriel.

Greg told him he was good friends with Father Christmas and had spoken to him about a special present for Gabriel. Then Greg gave Gabriel the bike, a beautiful silver bike.

And Gabriel rode round and round and round . . .

Selected Discography

Greg Lake's solo and group albums including both the studio and the principal live releases. (NB The list does not include the vast range of compilations, reissues, overseas-only releases, official bootlegs, unofficial bootlegs or singles.)

King Crimson
Studio:

In the Court of the Crimson King (1969)

'21st Century Schizoid Man' (including 'Mirrors')

'I Talk to the Wind'

'Epitaph' (including 'March for No Reason'; 'Tomorrow and Tomorrow')

'Moonchild' (including 'The Dream'; 'The Illusion')

'The Court of the Crimson King' (including 'The Return of the Fire Witch'; 'The Dance of the Puppets')

In the Wake of Poseidon (1970)

'Peace – A Beginning'

'Pictures of a City' (including '42nd at Treadmill')

'Cadence and Cascade'

'In the Wake of Poseidon' (including 'Libra's Theme')

'Peace – A Theme'

'Cat Food'

'The Devil's Triangle' (including I 'Merday Morn'; II 'Hand of Sceiron'; III 'Garden of Worm')

'Peace – An End'

Live:

Epitaph (recorded 1969; released 1997)

Maida Vale Studios, 6 May 1969:

'21st Century Schizoid Man'

'The Court of the Crimson King'

'Get Thy Bearings'

'Epitaph'

Fillmore East, 21 November 1969:

'A Man, a City'

'21st Century Schizoid Man'

'The Court of the Crimson King'

Fillmore West, 14 December 1969:

'Mantra'

'Travel Weary Capricorn'

'Improv – Travel Bleary Capricorn'

'Mars'

Fillmore West, 15 December 1969:

'The Court of the Crimson King'

'Drop In'

'A Man, a City'

'Epitaph'

'21st Century Schizoid Man'

'Mars'

Ninth National Jazz and Blues Festival, 9 August 1969:

'21st Century Schizoid Man'

'Get Thy Bearings'

'The Court of the Crimson King'

'Mantra'

'Travel Weary Capricorn'

'Improv' (including 'By the Sleeping Lagoon')

'Mars'

Chesterfield Jazz Club, 7 September 1969:

'21st Century Schizoid Man'

'Drop In'

'Epitaph'

'Get Thy Bearings'

'Mantra'

'Travel Weary Capricorn'

'Improv'

'Mars'

Emerson, Lake & Palmer

Studio:

Emerson, Lake & Palmer (1970)

'The Barbarian'

'Take a Pebble'

'Knife-Edge'

'The Three Fates' (including 'Clotho'; 'Lachesis'; 'Atropos')

'Tank'

'Lucky Man'

Tarkus (1971)

'Tarkus' (including 'Eruption';
    'Stones of Years'; 'Iconoclast';
    'Mass'; 'Manticore';
    'Battlefield'; 'Aquatarkus')

'Jeremy Bender'

'Bitches Crystal'

'The Only Way (Hymn)'

'Infinite Space (Conclusion)'

'A Time and a Place'

'Are You Ready Eddy?'

Trilogy (1972)

'The Endless Enigma (Part One)'

'Fugue'

'The Endless Enigma
    (Part Two)'

'From the Beginning'

'The Sheriff'

'Hoedown'

'Trilogy'

'Living Sin'

'Abaddon's Bolero'

Brain Salad Surgery (1973)

'Jerusalem'

'Toccata'

'Still . . . You Turn Me On'

'Benny the Bouncer'

'Karn Evil 9: 1st Impression –
    Part 1'

'Karn Evil 9: 1st Impression –
    Part 2'

'Karn Evil 9: 2nd Impression'

'Karn Evil 9: 3rd Impression'

Works Volume 1 (1977)

'Piano Concerto No. 1' (including
    'First Movement: Allegro
    Giojoso'; 'Second Movement:
    Andante Molto Cantibile';
    'Third Movement: Toccata con
    Fuoco')

'Lend Your Love to Me Tonight'

'C'est la Vie'

'Hallowed Be Thy Name'

'Nobody Loves You Like I Do'

'Closer to Believing'

'The Enemy God Dances with the
    Black Spirits'

'L.A. Nights'

'New Orleans'

'Two Part Invention in D Minor'

'Food for Your Soul'

'Tank'

'Fanfare for the Common Man'

'Pirates'

Works Volume 2 (1977)

'Tiger in a Spotlight'

'When the Apple Blossoms Bloom
    in the Windmills of Your Mind
    I'll Be Your Valentine'

'Bullfrog'
'Brain Salad Surgery'
'Barrelhouse Shake-Down'
'Watching Over You'
'So Far to Fall'
'Maple Leaf Rag'
'I Believe in Father Christmas'
'Close But Not Touching'
'Honky Tonk Train Blues'
'Show Me the Way to Go
    Home'

Love Beach (1978)
'All I Want Is You'
'Love Beach'
'Taste of My Love'
'The Gambler'
'For You'
'Canario'
'Memoirs of an Officer and a
    Gentleman' (including 'Prologue/
    The Education of a Gentleman';
    'Love at First Sight'; 'Letters
    from the Front'; 'Honourable
    Company
    (A March)')

Black Moon (1992)
'Black Moon'
'Paper Blood'
'Affairs of the Heart'
'Romeo and Juliet'

'Farwell to Arms'
'Changing States'
'Burning Bridges'
'Close to Home'
'Better Days'
'Footprints in the Snow'

In the Hot Seat (1994)
'Hand of Truth'
'Daddy'
'One by One'
'Heart on Ice'
'Thin Line'
'Man in the Long Coat'
'Change'
'Give Me a Reason to Stay'
'Gone Too Soon'
'Street War'

Live:

Pictures at an Exhibition (recorded
    at Newcastle City Hall,
    Newcastle, 26 March 1971;
    released 1971)
'Promenade'
'The Gnome'
'Promenade'
'The Sage'
'The Old Castle'
'Blues Variation'
'Promenade'

'The Hut of Baba Yaga'

'The Curse of Baba Yaga'

'The Hut of Baba Yaga'

'The Great Gates of Kiev'

'Nutrocker'

Welcome Back, My Friends, to the Show that Never Ends — Ladies and Gentlemen (recorded at Anaheim Convention Center, Anaheim, CA, 10 February 1974; released 1974)

'Hoedown'

'Jerusalem'

'Toccata'

'Tarkus' (including 'Eruption'; 'Stones of Years'; 'Iconoclast'; 'Mass'; 'Manticore'; 'Battlefield' [including 'Epitaph']; 'Aquatarkus')

'Take a Pebble' (including 'Still . . . You Turn Me On'; 'Lucky Man')

'Piano Improvisations' (including 'Fugue'; 'Little Rock Getaway')

'Take a Pebble (Conclusion)'

'Jeremy Bender/The Sheriff'

'Karn Evil 9: 1st Impression'

'Karn Evil 9: 2nd Impression'

'Karn Evil 9: 3rd Impression'

Emerson, Lake & Palmer in Concert (recorded at the Olympic Stadium, Montreal, 26 August 1977; released 1979)

'Introductory Fanfare'

'Peter Gunn'

'Tiger in a Spotlight'

'C'est la Vie'

'The Enemy God Dances with the Black Spirits'

'Knife-Edge'

'Piano Concerto No. 1, Third Movement: Toccata con Fuoco'

'Pictures at an Exhibition'

Live at the Royal Albert Hall (recorded at the Royal Albert Hall, London, 3 October 1992; released 1993)

'Karn Evil 9: 1st Impression — Part 2'

'Tarkus' (including 'Eruption'; 'Stones of Years'; 'Iconoclast')

'Knife-Edge'

'Paper Blood'

'Romeo and Juliet'

'Creole Dance'

'Still . . . You Turn Me On'

'Lucky Man'

'Black Moon'

'Pirates'

'Finale (Medley)' (including 'Fanfare for the Common Man'; 'America'; 'Rondo')

High Voltage (recorded at Victoria Park, London, 25 July 2010; released 2010)

'Karn Evil 9: 1st Impression – Part 2'

'The Barbarian'

'Bitches Crystal'

'Knife-Edge'

'From the Beginning'

'Touch and Go'

'Take a Pebble / Tarkus'

'Farwell to Arms'

'Lucky Man'

'Pictures at an Exhibition'

'Fanfare for the Common Man / Drum Solo / Rondo'

Greg Lake

Studio:

Greg Lake (1981)

'Nuclear Attack'

'Love You Too Much'

'It Hurts'

'Black and Blue'

'Retribution Drive'

'Long Goodbye'

'The Lie'

'Someone'

'Let Me Love You Once Before You Go'

'For Those Who Dare'

Manoeuvres (1983)

'Manoeuvres'

'Too Young to Love'

'Paralysed'

'A Woman Like You'

'I Don't Want to Lose Your Love Tonight'

'It's You, You've Gotta Believe'

'Famous Last Words'

'Slave to Love'

'Haunted'

'I Don't Know Why I Still Love You'

Live:

King Biscuit Flower Hour Presents Greg Lake in Concert (recorded at Hammersmith Odeon, London, 5 November 1981; released 1995)

'Fanfare for the Common Man'

'Karn Evil 9'

'Nuclear Attack'

'The Lie'

'Retribution Drive'

'Lucky Man'

'Parisienne Walkways'

'You've Really Got a Hold on Me'

'Love You Too Much'

'21st Century Schizoid Man'

'The Court of the Crimson King'

Greg Lake: Live (recorded 2005; released 2007)

'The Court of the Crimson King'

'Paper Blood'

'From the Beginning'

'Touch and Go'

'Take a Pebble'

'I Believe in Father Christmas'

'Farewell to Arms'

'Fanfare for the Common Man'

'Love You Too Much'

'Footprints in the Snow'

'Lucky Man'

'21st Century Schizoid Man'

'Pictures at an Exhibition'

'Karn Evil 9: 1st Impression – Part 2'

Songs of a Lifetime (recorded 2012; released 2013)

'21st Century Schizoid Man'

'Lend Your Love to Me Tonight'

'Songs of a Lifetime Tour Introduction'

'From the Beginning'

'Tribute to the King'

'Heartbreak Hotel'

'Epitaph / The Court of the Crimson King'

'King Crimson Cover Story'

'I Talk to the Wind'

'Ringo and the Beatles'

'You've Got to Hide Your Love Away'

'Touch and Go'

'Trilogy'

'Still . . . You Turn Me On'

'Reflections of Paris'

'C'est la Vie'

'My Very First Guitar'

'Lucky Man'

'People Get Ready'

'Karn Evil 9: 1st Impression – Part 2'

Asia

Live:

Ensŏ' Kai (recorded at the Nippon Budokan, Tokyo, 6 December 1983; released 2001)

'The Heat Goes On'

'Here Comes the Feeling'

'Eye to Eye'

'Only Time Will Tell'

'Open Your Eyes'

'Untitled'

'The Smile Has Left Your Eyes'

'Wildest Dreams'

'Heat of the Moment'

'Sole Survivor'

Emerson, Lake & Powell
Studio:
Emerson, Lake & Powell (1986)
'The Score'
'Learning to Fly'
'The Miracle'
'Touch and Go'
'Love Blind'
'Step Aside'
'Lay Down Your Guns'
'Mars, the Bringer of War'

Live:
Emerson, Lake & Powell Live in Concert and More . . . (recorded 1986; released 2012)
Live in Concert, Lakeland, Florida, November 1986:
'The Score'
'Touch and Go'
'Knife-Edge'
'Pirates'
'From the Beginning'
'Lucky Man'
'Fanfare for the Common Man'
'Mars, the Bringer of War/Drum Solo'
'Karn Evil 9: 1st Impression/ America/Rondo'
The Sprocket Sessions, rehearsals, 1986:
'The Score'

'Learning to Fly'
'The Miracle'
'Knife-Edge'
'Tarkus'
'Pictures at an Exhibition'
'Lucky Man (Excerpt)'
'Still . . . You Turn Me On'
'Love Blind'
'Mars, the Bringer of War'
'Touch and Go'
'Pirates'

Greg Lake & Geoff Downes
Studio:
Ride the Tiger (recorded 1988; released 2015)
'Money Talks'
'Love Under Fire'
'Affairs of the Heart'
'Street Wars'
'Check It Out'
'Blue Light'
'Love Under Fire' (alt. mix)

Ringo Starr and His New All-Starr Band
Live:
King Biscuit Flower Hour Presents Ringo Starr and His New All-Starr Band (recorded Rosemont Theatre, Rosemont, IL, 22 August 2001; released 2002)

'Photograph'

'Act Naturally'

'Logical Song'

'No One Is to Blame'

'Yellow Submarine'

'Give a Little Bit'

'You're Sixteen'

'The No-No Song'

'Back Off Boogaloo'

'Glamorous Life'

'I Wanna Be Your Man'

'Lucky Man'

'Take the Long Way Home'

'All the Young Dudes'

'Don't Go Where the Road Don't Go'

'With a Little Help from My Friends'

Keith Emerson & Greg Lake

Live:

Live from Manticore Hall (recorded 2010; released 2014)

'From the Beginning'

'Introduction'

'I Talk to the Wind'

'Bitches Crystal'

'The Barbarian'

'Take a Pebble'

'Tarkus'

'C'est la Vie'

'Pirates'

'Moog Solo / Lucky Man'